Are There Black Neighborhoods in Heaven?

George Smith

PEGASUS BOOKS
Copyright © 2025 George Smith
All Rights Reserved

Copyright © 2025 by George Smith

All Rights Reserved. No part of this book may be produced or transmitted in any form or by any means, electronic or mechanical, including photocopying, recording or by an information storage and retrieval system—except by a reviewer who may quote brief passages in a review to be printed in a magazine or newspaper—without permission in writing from the publisher.

Pegasus Books
8165 Valley Green Drive
Sacramento, CA 95820
www.pegasusbooks.net

Second Edition: January 2025
Published in North America by Pegasus Books. For information, please contact Pegasus Books c/o Marcus McGee, 8165 Valley Green Drive, Sacramento, CA 95823.

Library of Congress Cataloguing-In-Publication Data
George Smith
Are There Black Neighborhoods in Heaven? / George Smith – 2nd ed
p. cm.
Library of Congress Control Number: 2020952557
ISBN – 978-1-941859-93-3

1. BIOGRAPHY & AUTOBIOGRAPHY / African American & Black 2. HISTORY / African American & Black. 3. SOCIAL SCIENCE / Cultural & Ethnic Studies / American / African American & Black Studies. 4. EDUCATION / Leadership

10   9   8   7   6   5   4   3   2

Comments about *Are There Black Neighborhoods in Heaven?* and requests for additional copies, book club rates and author speaking appearances may be addressed to George Smith via e-mail to grishama@gmail.com
Also available as an eBook from Internet retailers and from Pegasus Books

Printed in the United States of America

Dedication

This book is dedicated to my late son,
Marcus Allan Smith, Mark (1976-2019).

For me, one of the most challenging aspects of being a Black father was knowing when and how often to warn my children about the various forms of racism they were likely to encounter in their lives. As a Black man, I had experienced a fair amount of racism in my life, but the more I tried to talk to Mark about what he could expect in terms of race, the more he pushed back, no doubt confident that he would overcome racism. I was careful not to overreact to Mark's resistance, remembering how I had acted when I was his age and my father, who was a son of the segregated Jim Crow South, was constantly in my ear about racism. I realized that Mark saw me as being as "old fashioned" as I had once regarded my father.

But I was determined that I would never let a potentially racist situation that could adversely affect Mark pass without saying something to him about it, whether he wanted to hear it or not.

I loved it when Mark was an adult and I mentioned to him that his mother and I were considering a move to another city, and he told me, "I don't know if that'd be a good place for you and Mom. I've been there and I noticed how some of those White folks were watching me." And then he laughed.

Preface

What does the above cartoon depict?
A. Affirmative Action
B. Black Lives Matter
C. Black Power
D. Civil Rights
E. Counter Culture
F. Critical Race Theory
G. Diversity
H. White Supremacy
I. Wokeness
J. All of the Above
K. None of the Above

Explain your answer.

If I were still teaching Human Resource Management to B-school students, as I once did, I would ask them to answer that question, to the best of their ability. It's hard. Race is complicated. Race means something different to each of us.

ARE THERE BLACK NEIGHBORHOODS IN HEAVEN?

Contents

"Truth" ……………………………………………………...1
"Suite Malcolm" ……………………………………………… 3
…*Her name was Miss Rudolph. You know they named her after that deer.* ……………………………………………… 12
"When I see an Elephant fly" …………………………………. 16
"Stompin' At the Savoy" ……………………………………… 19
"Money Honey" ………………………………………………23
"I'm Gone" …………………………………………………… 27
"My Only Love" ………………………………………………30
"Life could be a dream… life could be a dream…" …………… 32
"Did You See Jackie Robinson Hit That Ball?" …………………36
"Why Do You Have to Go" …………………………………… 41
"Whispering Bells" …………………………………………... 44
"It's All in the Game" …………………………………………47
"Tears On My Pillow" ………………………………………… 49
"Will You Still Love Me Tomorrow" ………………………… 53
"For many years I was the glory of Chicago's Southside
I lived the life of the hip, thrilling to Coltrane's saxophone
And spoke a coded language Only the hip could understand" … 55
"Let's Go, Let's Go, Let's Go" ………………………………… 58
"Am I Fooling Myself Again"   61
"Dancing is alright. But you can have a good time without dancing. Dancing won't make you cry. Crying is a strong emotion." …… 64
"I'll Try Something New" ……………………………………. 68
"Do You Love Me" …………………………………………… 71
"Surfin' USA" ………………………………………………… 74
"Freedom Sound" ……………………………………………… 77
"(Nobody oughta be) Alone at Christmas" ……………………79
"Saturday Morning" …………………………………………… 84
"How Can I Forget?" …………………………………………87
"Come and Get These Memories" ……………………………90
"Found True Love" …………………………………………… 92
"Miss Ann" …………………………………………………… 96
"A Love Supreme" …………………………………………… 99
"Again" ……………………………………………………… 101
"Footprints" ………………………………………………… 103
"He'll Be Back" ……………………………………………… 105
"This Love" ………………………………………………… 109
"Since I Lost My Baby" ……………………………………… 113

"But It's Alright"	116
"2, 4, 6, 8! We don't want to integrate!" "14, 12, 10, 8! you will, or you won't graduate!!"	120
"Happenings"	124
"Get Ready"	126
"Mode for Joe"	130
"Groovin"	134
"Funky Broadway"	137
"Respect"	139
"Listen Here"	143
"The Inflated Tear"	146
"We're A Winner"	150
"It's A Beautiful Morning"	153
"Beginnings"	156
"Shopping for Clothes"	159
"Is It Because I'm Black"	161
"Blasé"	163
"Everywhere"	165
"Thank You (Falettinme Be Mice Elf Agin)"	168
"Too Late to Turn Back Now"	170
"Just My Imagination"	172
"What's Going On"	174
"Shining Star"	176
"Flowers for Albert"	178
"Wantu Wazuri, Use Afro Sheen…Beautiful People, Use Afro Sheen"	181
"…You one of them technical niggas…You'll have problems here"	184
"By the time you realize that your father was right, you'll have a son of your own..."	188
"Rag, Bush and All"	191
"One line, Two views"	192
"Wayne's Trane"	195
"Beware Greeks bearing gifts, colored men asking for a loan and white men who understand the Negro."	198
"If I Break"	201
"Pastime Paradise"	204
"September"	207

—1—

"Truth"
Kamasi Washington

On a frosty, Indiana morning in October of 2008, I stepped out my house and paused, briefly, to breathe in the invigorating, morning air, and then I walked to the edge of my front yard to retrieve my daily newspaper. I was struck by the peacefulness. My wife, Gloria, and I really liked our house and the quiet neighborhood in which we lived in Indianapolis, despite our not having much interaction with our neighbors, all of whom were White. In the more than five years that we lived on the Southeast side of Indianapolis near the Geist Reservoir, only a few of our neighbors had been friendly.

The Presidential election was only a month away, and before I went back inside, I glanced up and down the block and realized that several of my neighbors had put "Vote for..." signs in their well-manicured front lawns. Reading the "Vote for..." signs in two of the yards, doors from my house. The signs in those yards read "Obama/Biden." How had I missed the fact that at least two of my White neighbors, neither of whom had ever said so much as "hello" to me or Gloria, were openly supporting Barack Obama, a Black man, for President of the United States. Had I been too hung up on *race* to notice that I was amongst friends in this mostly White community?

After getting past the initial shock of seeing that some of my White neighbors were planning to vote for Barack Obama, I concluded that it was time for me to re-examine my cynicism about race and the nature of racism. As a result of my "new thinking," I began going out of my way to be the bigger person and reach out more to my White neighbors — nothing over the top, just an occasional wave or a "Good morning" whenever our paths crossed in the neighborhood. Usually, I got "Good mornings" right back, which I interpreted as a sign that the dynamics of Black people living in mostly all-White enclaves might be changing.

Later that same week, I experienced another reality. On a mild October evening as I was driving home down a remote street in the neighborhood, I saw a White female jogger out of the corner of my eye, emerging from a wooded area, on a course to cross in front of me. It was a beautiful autumn evening, and feeling malice toward none, I slowed to a complete stop, smiled and waved the jogger across the street. The jogger continued looking straight ahead, never acknowledging my gesture of kindness with a wave or a nod and, in a voice loud enough for me to hear through my partially opened window, she hissed, "I'm the boss! You're not the boss!" before disappearing into the woods on the other side of the road.

What was that? Did the White female jogger think that I was being "fresh with her" when I stopped and waved her across the road? Was she reacting to the realization that Barack Obama was about to become "the boss?" Was she simply paranoid? White folks are often schizophrenic when it comes to race. I have ancestors who were a mixed-race couple in the early 19th century who were listed in one census as "White," and then, ten years later, they were listed as "Mulatto," and ten years after that, as "Black." White people recorded those censuses. Race has baffled White people for centuries.

The election of Barack Obama as President of the United States brought on the same reaction among White folks as that white jogger I encountered. Obama's election to President of the United States was a sign that the days of assuming that White people would always be "the boss" of everything were over. It is a difficult adjustment for many White people, because they have been raised to believe that Black people are inferior. That is the legacy of slavery. There are more White people who see Black people as inferior then there are White people who see themselves as superior to Black people. White people object to being labeled a "White supremacists," because it makes them sound racist.

—2—

"Suite Malcolm"
Don Pullen

I once saw a list of the "25 Coolest Brothers of All Time." Dr. Martin Luther King was not on that list. Malcolm X was. Malcolm X had been a hero of Black people of my generation. So in 1982, when I heard that Alex Haley, the author of the *Autobiography of Malcolm X*, would be speaking in nearby Evanston, Illinois, I left work early and drove to Evanston. Malcolm X was the inspirational Black leader of my generation, and because I had so thoroughly enjoyed Haley's book, I was eager to hear Haley talk about Malcolm X's legacy, especially since racial injustices were as much of an issue in 1982 as they had been in 1965, when Malcolm X was killed.

To my surprise, Haley barely mentioned Malcolm X during his speech that day in Evanston. Instead, Haley talked about how he had been inspired to research his family's genealogy, from his African roots and slave ancestry to the present, a saga that culminated in his best-selling novel and blockbuster TV mini-series, *Roots*. Early in his remarks, Haley referred to a time when he was speaking somewhere in the Midwest, when a White man in the audience told the author that he was a descendant of the White

My father, George O. Smith

family that had once owned Haley's enslaved ancestors. The concept of learning about my roots captured my imagination. At the time, I had not read *Roots* or watched the TV movie, but listening to Haley was riveting, and the idea of trying to trace my own roots was implanted in my brain. I could hardly wait to get started on my search.

Ancestry.com did not exist in 1982 and genealogy was a formidable undertaking, especially for Black people, whose ancestors were often slaves, without last names. But, with both my parents and my grandfather still alive and sound of mind, I was optimistic that there might be a chance that I could trace my roots back to the time when my ancestors had been brought to America from Africa, enslaved and eventually freed.

I began my search by asking my father, George Oliver Smith, what he knew about our family's ancestry, confident that he would have much to say, since he talked about race all the time when I was growing up in the 1950s. Dad was born in Tennessee in 1911, and he always talked about race and Black history. When I asked him to share our family's roots, he said, "All I know is that, when I was a kid, I was told that my grandfather had been a slave. And when he was freed, he told people that he did not want the slave master's name… 'just call me Smith!'" After thinking about it, I decided that trying to trace a name as common as *Smith* might be difficult, so I decided to start the search for my roots on my mother's side of the family, where the uncommon last name was "Artis."

When I asked my mother, Lorrine Artis Smith what she knew about our roots, she said she did not know very much because she and her twin sister, Corrine, always tried to avoid "those Artis Family Reunions that Pop (their father) would make us attend." "The best way to find out about our roots," Mom laughed, "is to go down to Springfield and ask Pop, your grandfather." So that is what I did.

Are There Black Neighborhoods in Heaven?

When I was a little boy, my grandfather entertained me often with stories about our family's history, but I always thought of those stories as adventure stories, not history. For example, Grandpa told me stories about how his grandfather, Henry Artis, had served in the Union Army's Colored Troops in the Civil War, where he was called "Cap'n" by the other Black soldiers because he had taken charge of the company when the White commanding officer was killed in action.

As a kid, I liked war stories and, as my grandfather was telling me stories about his grandfather, I tried to imagine my great-great grandfather, Henry Artis, commanding those troops, with gunfire and cannonballs exploding around him.

Grandpa also told me about the time that the notorious outlaw, Jesse James, robbed a bank in Missouri, where his mother, Georgeanne Artis, was working. Grandpa reminded me of how Great Grandma used to show me and my cousins the bank manager's old, bloodstained shirt whenever we visited her at her home in Lincoln, Illinois. Grandpa also told me about the time, as a Mortician's Apprentice in Chicago during Chicago's Race Riot of 1919, he saved a man from a marauding mob by hiding the man inside a coffin. I forgot to ask my grandfather if the man he saved was Black or White.

When I arrived at my grandfather's house in Springfield, Illinois, he led me into a cluttered room, with papers strewn everywhere. He told me he was looking for a copy of our family's coat of arms. "When I found out you were coming, I wanted to have that coat of arms to show you," Grandpa said. I tried to explain to my grandfather that I was not as interested in learning about a European coat of arms as I was about our African roots and slavery. With a confused look on his face, Grandpa muttered, "Why would anybody want to know about Africa?"

Grandpa sat down in his big, easy chair and I turned on a tape recorder. "Start wherever you like," I told him, and with a twinkle in his eye, he started talking. The Cliff's Notes version of what he told me went something like this:

> "The Artis men come from a long line of free Black men. Our clan started in the year 17-something in North Carolina, when a merchant and his wife came to America from Germany. The merchant and his wife brought with them a White, indentured

servant girl and settled on 166 acres near Snow Hill, North Carolina. When the merchant and his wife died, the indentured servant became free, and, since the merchant and his wife had no children of their own, the newly freed servant inherited the merchant's 166 acres.

The former White indentured servant did not inherit any slaves, and since she needed help in working the land she had inherited, she rented Black slaves from a neighboring plantation. Eventually, the former indentured servant became involved with one of the slaves she was renting, whose last name was already Artis.

My great-great-great Grandfather, Reverend Lewis Artis, born free in 1811 near Snow Hill, North Carolina, was founder and first pastor of the Missionary Baptist Church in Lost Creek, Indiana in 1850.

When the man who owned the slave called Artis wanted to add the former servant's 166 acres to his own plantation, he made her an offer for her land. The former servant asked him to include the freedom of the slave named Artis in the land sale, and the plantation owner agreed.

The former slave and the White, former indentured servant married and eventually left North Carolina in covered wagons, along with other free Blacks. The free Blacks in the covered wagons settled in Canada, Ohio, Cass County, Michigan and Indiana. The former slave called Artis and the White, ex-indentured servant settled in Lost Creek, Indiana, a Quaker settlement connected with the Underground Railroad. The Artis clan gradually moved into Illinois."

That is as far as my grandfather was able to go but I started doing my own research and found that free Artis born to the ex-slave and the White ex-indentured servant, Lewis Artis, was born in North Carolina in 1811. He founded a church in Lost Creek,

Indiana, in 1850 and eventually died in Charleston, Illinois, in 1866. Lewis's son, Henry, my grandfather's grandfather, was born free in North Carolina in 1835, served in the Union Army's 28th Colored Troops out of Indiana, and he became a barber, settling in Paris, Illinois, where he lived to be 100, dying in 1935.

(Right to left) My great, great grandfather, Henry Artis, born "free" in 1835 in North Carolina; great grandfather, Thomas Artis, born "free" in 1864 in Indiana; my grandfather, Orville Artis, born in 1892 in Lincoln, Illinois; my uncle, D'Arcy Artis, born 1914 in Buffalo Hart, Illinois.

Henry's son, Thomas, my grandfather's father and Georgeanne's husband, was born in Indiana. My grandfather, Orville, was born in 1893 in Lincoln, Illinois, and finally, my mother, Lorrine Artis, and her twin sister, Corrine, were born in 1915 in Buffalo Hart, Illinois, just outside Springfield, Illinois. I, myself, was born in Springfield in 1944, when my mother went home to Springfield during WWII, when my father was overseas in the Navy.

After learning about my roots from my grandfather, I did more research and discovered free Black Artis family members in North Carolina, dating back to 1687. I think it would help White people understand race better if they were to take a close look at some Black person's roots. White people should think of it as learning more about American history rather than Black history.

Only the residents whose names were recorded in a census were "free" men and women. Joseph Artis and his wife Sarah are both listed as "white" in the 1850 Census (lines 10 and 11), "mulatto" in the 1860 Census (next page - lines 13 and 14) and Black in the 1870 Census (page after next - lines 34 and 35). See how complicated race can be?

Are There Black Neighborhoods in Heaven?

My great-great grandfather, Henry Artis, fought in the Civil War in this unit, the 28th Regiment of US Colored Troops out of Indiana. I can't tell if Henry is in this picture but the 28th Regiment of the USCT fought in the Siege at Petersburgh, Virginia, in 1864, including the Battle of the Crater, in which the 28th suffered huge losses. Henry Artis survived, and at one point he was called upon to command troops, earning him the nickname, "Cap'n," Henry lived to be 99 years old and died in Paris, Illinois, in 1935.

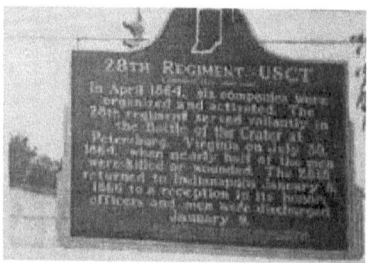

My great grandmother, Georgeanne Artis, who was once robbed by notorious outlaw Jesse James, while working at a bank in Missouri. James shot and wounded her boss, the bank manager

My father (in the car) with his siblings in 1913 in Nashville, Tennessee.

The Artis twins in 1915 and the Artis twins in 2015. My mother, Lorrine, is on the left, and my Aunt Corrine is on the right, in both pictures. The twins' 100th birthday cake.

— 3 —

"...Her name was Miss Rudolph.
You know they named her after that deer."
Richard Pryor

Having a father who talked about race all the time and a grandfather who could recall our family's history, dating back to slavery, one could conclude that I probably grew up with race on my mind, virtually from birth. But that is not the way racial awareness happened with me at all. I know the exact time and place when I began to pay attention to race: It was on Friday, December 22, 1950. I was six years old. I had been hearing grownups talk about race, but it was not until Christmas of 1950 that it started to mean something to me. Here is how it happened.

My father's cramped little tailor shop and dry cleaners in the basement of the building was always busy at Christmas time, and December of 1950 was no exception. We lived at 4105 South Indiana Avenue, on Chicago's all-Black Southside. My father, George O. Smith, was a tailor, and at Christmas, he always seemed to be hunched over a sewing machine in the tiny little shop, made steamier by the press machine that both he and my mother operated.

During Christmas season, my mother would work next to my father in the shop, sliding in and out of the tightly packed rows of bagged garments, looking to match a customer's claim check to the tag on the bag. The closer it got to Christmas, the more folks from the neighborhood would bring clothes into the shop to be cleaned and pressed or patched.

There was not enough space in the shop for me and my four-year-old sister, Janice to play, so when things got busy in the shop, my mother would leave Janice and me upstairs, where the Jones family and their teenage daughter, Bobbye, would watch me and my sister. Mom often hired Bobbye whenever she needed someone to babysit my sister and me and, with her working in the shop so much in the days leading up to Christmas time, my sister and I got used to spending time with Bobbye.

Despite the Christmas Holidays always being a very busy time in the shop, my mother never failed to find time to take my sister and I downtown on the "L train" to a department store to see Santa Claus, so that we could tell Santa what we wanted for Christmas. Mom kept one of those Christmas calendars that you peel open each day, leading up to December 25, so I always knew exactly how many days there were until December 24th, Christmas Eve, my last chance to tell Santa what I wanted for Christmas.

When the calendar read December 19th and I still had not been downtown to see Santa, a sense of panic came over me. With only five days left before Christmas Eve, my mother still had not taken me downtown to see Santa, so I decided I had better remind my mother. Mom said, "I know. Don't worry. You'll get your chance to talk with Santa." And. sure enough, early the next morning, right after eating my cereal, Mom said, "Hurry and get ready because, Bobbye's taking you and your sister to see Santa Claus."

I bolted from the table, put on my coat and started helping my sister put on her boots. Minutes later, Bobbye came bounding downstairs, already dressed for the outdoors. She finished buttoning my sister's coat and we were out the door, on our way to see Santa. As soon as we left the house, however, I noticed that Bobbye was not going downtown, the usual way. We walked east, to South Park Boulevard, where Bobbye flagged a jitney cab heading south. We took the jitney to 47th and South Park, where Bobbye whisked us into South Center Department Store, which the people in my neighborhood called the "Colored Store" because all the salesclerks were "colored."

Whenever my father heard someone refer to South Center as the Colored Store, he would correct them and say, "South Center is owned by white people...colored people just work there." Mom seldom shopped at South Center. "Because" she would complain, "I can never find what I'm looking for at South Center like I can at the stores downtown."

One time, earlier in the year, when Bobbye was supposed to be taking my sister and me to the movies, she stopped first at South Center to pay on a layaway bill. On that day, I figured that we were briefly stopping at South Center so that Bobbye could pay on her bill and then we would head downtown to see Santa. But once inside the store, Bobbye led us to a long line of children and adults, next to a sign that read, "To Santa," and an arrow pointing the way.

I leaned out of the line to get a better vantage point and saw the Great Man seated in a grand chair. I could not believe my eyes and I looked again. The Santa Claus awaiting me at the end of the line was Black!

The Negro Santa Claus was stout, had a white beard, a big, red Santa Claus suit and he ho-ho-ho-ed so loud that I could hear him all the way at the back of the line, just like I used to hear the White Santa's downtown. When my little sister saw the Negro Santa Claus, her eyes grew wide, and she clamped desperately onto Bobbye's leg. In the meanwhile, I was so eager to tell Santa—any Santa—what I wanted for Christmas, I waited patiently in line, my eyes affixed to the strange sight of a Negro Santa Claus.

When our turn finally came, my sister would not let go of Bobbye's leg and move ahead, so I deftly stepped around her, rushed up to the Negro Santa Claus and scrambled up on to his knee. Before the Black Santa could even ask me "What would you like Santa to bring you?" I rattled off the names of the two toys that I most wanted for Christmas. (My mother always told my sister and me never to ask Santa for more than two toys, so there would be enough toys for all the children in the World.) I was also told that Santa Claus delivered the two toys that I knew my sister wanted. We left South Center right after seeing Santa, and I was in a daze all the way home.

As soon as we got back home, I ran into the shop and shouted, "Mom, Bobbye took us to South Center... and we saw a colored Santa Claus!"

My mother opened her mouth to speak but Dad beat her to the punch. "All those Santa Clauses you see in stores at Christmas, even the ones downtown, are just Santa Claus' helpers. They tell the real Santa at the North Pole what toys kids want and the real Santa brings the toys on Christmas morning."

At the time, I bought my father's explanation, but I did not think to ask him if the "real Santa" was Black or White. At first, I was surprised to hear my father say that the White Santas were Santa's helpers too, but the longer I thought about it, the more sense it made.

The very next day, my mother took me and my sister downtown on the "L," to see the Santa Claus in Wieboldt's Department Store. As usual, the Santa at Wieboldt's was White. My sister did not hesitate to walk right up to the White Santa Claus and tell him what she wanted for Christmas. For the record, I asked the White Santa Claus at Wieboldt's for the exact same two toys that I had asked the Black Santa Claus for at South Center. When both toys showed up under our Christmas tree on Christmas morning, I stopped worrying about whether the Black Santa Claus was real, although I did wonder why I had never seen a Black Santa's helper at any of the department stores downtown.

I got over the shock of seeing that chocolate-colored Santa Claus in no time. What did stay with me, though, was the concern my mother exhibited when I mentioned the Black Santa. The very next day, Mom took me and my sister downtown where we saw a White Santa. I asked the White Santa for the same two toys I asked the Black Santa for and, when those two toys showed up under the Christmas tree on Christmas morning, I did not give the Black Santa much more thought. That was my introduction to race.

After years of seeing only White Santas, what was to make of seeing a Black Santa. It was my first "race" moment.

Credit: the Amos 'n' Andy "Christmas Story" from 1952, with actor Spencer Williams as Andy Brown, dressed as the Black Santa Claus and a kid named Baxter Rosebarr as the little boy talking with Santa.

— 4 —

"When I See an Elephant Fly"
Cliff Edwards/The Hall Johnson Choir

My next "race moment" occurred less than a year after seeing that colored Santa Claus. My mother took me to see the animated Walt Disney movie, Dumbo, about a baby elephant whose ears were so large he used them to fly like a bird. Expecting the usual, cute Disney fare that I had already seen like Snow White and The Seven Dwarfs, Pinocchio, Bambi and Cinderella, I settled down in the show to experience the Disney fantasy magic. So, you can imagine my reaction when The Crows made their appearance in Dumbo, sounding and acting just like Black people in my neighborhood, shuckin 'n' jivin and signifyin.

Growing up in the early 1950s, you almost never saw Black people on TV or in movies, not even in crowd scenes. And, on those rare occasions when you did see someone Black in a movie, the Black actor or actress would be in a small role, portraying a butler or a "mammie" figure like Beulah or they would be a child-like character like Buckwheat in the "Our Gang/Little Rascals" movies or Willie, the eye-rolling handyman portrayed by actor Willie Best in the Stu Erwin Show on TV.

In the movie, *Dumbo*, the baby elephant drinks water that has been spiked and when he awakens from a deep sleep, he finds himself up in a tree surrounded by The Black Crows and trying to figure out how he got up into the tree. When someone tells Dumbo that he may have flown up into the tree, the Crows laugh hysterically and mockingly, sing, "I've seen time fly... I've seen a horsefly... but I be done seed 'bout ever' thang when I see a' elephant fly!"

When I laughed out loud in the theater, my mother quickly shissed me. "You shouldn't laugh when they make fun of colored people," she whispered, "White folks make Negroes act silly and sound ignorant in the movies. They want people to think that all Negroes act like those Crows. But you've never heard our family sound like that, now, have you?" I had never thought about that before.

Black people "acting silly," as she put it, was a big deal to my mother. For example, whenever we walked past the group of Black men who hung on the corner outside the liquor store, Mom would jerk my arm and make me pick up the pace as we hurried past the group of men and causing me to miss the punch lines. My mother never let me listen to Amos 'n' Andy on the radio, either. When I learned that Amos 'n' Andy was created and portrayed by two White men, Freeman Gosden and Charles Correll, I could hardly believe it because they sounded Black.

I don't think the Crows would have bothered my father, even though one of the Crows was named "Jim." For the most part, Dad had no problem laughing at Black people, especially if Black people were gettin paid.

My second "race" moment was hearing those Crows in the Disney movie, "Dumbo," sounding like Black people I knew in my neighborhood.for actin foolish." Dad would have been right about the Crows in "Dumbo" because Black actors provided the voices for all the Crows, except for the one named Jim.

Even as a little kid, I was beginning to pick up on what my father often complained about how White people were so denigratory about colored people. Growing up, my neighborhood friends and I referred to ourselves as "colored"; grownups used the term "Negroes." Black people seldom referred to themselves as "Black." In fact, many of them considered "Black" derogatory. And nobody used the expression "African Americans"

Another racial incident that made an impression on me, occurred in 1951 when I was seven. Harvey Clark, a Black college graduate and WWII veteran, attempted to move his family into an apartment in Cicero, Illinois, an all-White community on the Southwest side of Chicago. The Clarks were threatened by a White mob and the apartment building was set afire. The National Guard was called out to put down the mob and more than 100 people were arrested. but the only person indicted was the owner of the apartment building for trying to rent to a Black family, in the first place.

—5—

"Stompin' At the Savoy"
Norman Granz Jam Session w/Flip Phillips, Dizzy Gillespie, et al

Unlike most of the folks in my neighborhood, my parents were, basically, first generation Northerners and somewhat different culturally from most of our neighbors. Mom had never lived in the South and Dad had only lived in the Jim Crow South until he was seven. My father was born near Nashville, Tennessee, but what he knew about the South he learned from his mother and older siblings and the Black people who were recent migrants from the South, living in "Bronzeville," Chicago's vibrant, all-Black, Southside community.

Despite not being raised in the South, my father was militant about race discrimination and situations like the case of Harvey Clark. Part of my father's militancy that I observed came, not only from being raised in a segregated Chicago but also his having been drafted into a segregated U.S. Navy in 1943 when he and my mother were trying to start a family and establish a business. During WWII, Black men in the Navy served only as stewards, cooks or laborers, in segregated units, commanded by White officers.

In 1944, 320 sailors, most of them Black serving as laborers, were killed when the munitions they were loading onto ships, headed to the Pacific Theater, exploded in Port Chicago, California. In the aftermath of the disaster, fifty Black seamen refused to load munitions without proper training.

My father in the Navy in 1943

Those fifty Black sailors were court martialed, convicted of mutiny and sentenced to fifteen years in prison and hard labor. Most of the fifty Black mutineers were subsequently released from prison in January 1946 but the entire matter and other race-related protests, is what led to the desegregation of the Navy in February 1946. My father had already been discharged from service when the Navy was finally desegregated. But he never got over the anger he felt being a laborer in a segregated Navy.

As a kid, I did not fully understand the significance of segregation, when my father would talk about his experiences in the Navy during WWII. As an adult, though, I once offered to send my mother and father to Hawaii, all expenses paid, for their 50th wedding anniversary, but Dad declined my offer, telling me he did not care if he ever saw Hawaii again.

My mother knew even less about the South than my father, even though her mother, my grandmother, Minnie, was from Kentucky. My mother was born in Buffalo Hart, Illinois, in 1915 and raised in nearby Springfield.

Dad made his suit, my mother's suit and my suit for Easter, 1951. My sister, Janice, wanted a dress.

Despite being "the land of Abraham Lincoln," Springfield had its own infamous racial history, including a bloody race riot in 1908. Springfield was the Capital of the State of Illinois but was, nevertheless, a segregated town. In fact, in 1933, my mother, and her twin sister, Corrine, were the first two Black people to graduate from Springfield High School. My mother did not talk as much about race as my father, but she was vigilant about "how you need to act around White folks."

Included in the ways in which my family was culturally different from many of our neighbors is that we almost never went to church unless it was for a wedding or a funeral. Weather permitting, Dad played golf every Sunday, which was the only day the shop was closed. He was the only man in our neighborhood who golfed. One of the shop's regular customers was Reverend Lewis Rawls who pastored Tabernacle Baptist Church, which was across the street from our house. I was in the shop one day, when Reverend Rawls brought clothes in to be cleaned.

"Brother Smith," Reverend Rawls asked my father, "am I going to see you in church this Sunday?"

Dad hemmed and hawed, then said, "Hmmm...this Sunday? I don't know about this Sunday..." his voice trailing off. And that was the end of the conversation.

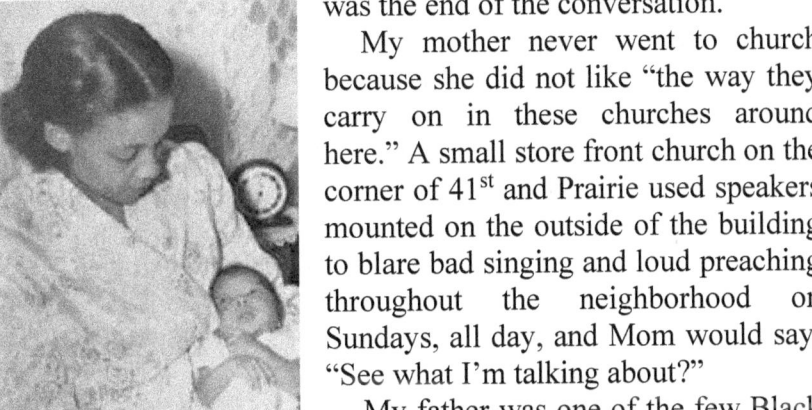

My mother never went to church because she did not like "the way they carry on in these churches around here." A small store front church on the corner of 41st and Prairie used speakers mounted on the outside of the building to blare bad singing and loud preaching throughout the neighborhood on Sundays, all day, and Mom would say, "See what I'm talking about?"

My father was one of the few Black businessmen in the neighborhood. He had learned tailoring from a Jewish tailor he worked for on the Northside of Chicago as a teenager. He and my mother started a tailoring and drycleaning business on 67th Street and lived in the back of the shop. Then, "Pearl Harbor" happened. When Dad got back from the War, he managed to use the GI Bill-type funding to finish tailoring school and earn a certificate.

My father built a reputation as one of the better tailors on Chicago's South Side. Not only was he making a lot of suits, at a time when Black men dressed up more, he also had a reputation as a "go-to tailor" for Black entertainers who were in Chicago to perform at popular South Side venues like the Savoy or the Palm Tavern and suddenly found themselves in need of last-minute repairs because of wardrobe malfunctions.

My folks never had a lot of what they would call "extra money," but they always managed to find money for those things they felt were important to me and my sister's development. When I was in nursery school, I started learning how to play piano. Eventually, my mother bought a cheap, third-hand piano and found a woman who gave my sister and me inexpensive piano lessons.

A few years later, when I got tired of taking music lessons on the piano, my mother let me take music lessons on a rented trumpet. And she found a way to pay for ballet lessons for my sister. I was always in The Boys Club or the Catholic Youth Organization or the Cub Scouts, to "keep me busy…and off the streets." On the other hand, we were the last family on the block to get a television set and my folks never let me have a bike or roller skates, arguing that "there isn't anywhere to ride a bike or skate on the sidewalk where people have to walk."

The summer when I was in CYO, a lot of my buddies in the neighborhood were developing "cool walks." I tried to have a cool walk, too, but my mother caught me "bopping" down the street, one day, and thumped me, telling me to "Walk like you got some sense!" My parents were serious, hard-working people. But they could also be cool, like the time I saw them "swinging out" to Count Basie's *One O'clock Jump*. It was awesome to watch.

Bobbye, my babysitter. Behind her, my cousin Marie, her father (my Uncle Johnny) and my father on our front porch @ 1951.

—6—

"Money Honey"
The Drifters

Kids on our front porch at 41st and Indiana Avenue in Chicago in 1955

My buddy, Ron Chears (second from the right) on the steps of Henry Horner School circa 1954

Another way in which my parents were different from our neighbors is that both of my parents were avid readers. Even though my father only went to the tenth grade, he loved reading. He read the newspaper from cover to cover, every day, including two Sunday newspapers. My father liked reading about current events, history, politics, natural history and science. I remember when he showed me an article in the newspaper about a "flying saucer" that had crashed in New Mexico.

The article he showed me was accompanied by an artist's drawing of an alien, which led to my father telling me all about Orson Welles' radio broadcast of The War of the Worlds about creatures from Mars. Looking back, I now think that the article my father showed me had to do with what became known as The Roswell Incident.

Thanks to being exposed to both my parents reading so much, I learned to read at a young age. In fact, by the time I entered Henry Horner Public School, across the street from my house, I was reading so much better than my classmates that I skipped two semesters. Being able to read enabled me to do well academically, but, sometimes, when I was not sufficiently challenged, my behavior in school would deteriorate.

Mostly, I was mouthy and, as a result, I received a grade of "unsatisfactory in conduct" on a few of my early report cards. My mother constantly expressed frustration that I was notworking up to my potential, while my father grumbled about me not taking advantage of my opportunity to go to school, reminding me of how he had to quit high school to help support his mother and siblings.

In 1953, when I was in fourth grade, my teacher, Miss Archer, assigned me to be a Hall Guard because, she said, "The added responsibility will be good for you and help you grow up." At first, I was proud to be Horner school's youngest Hall Guard, but I quickly lost my way. Early in my stint as a Hall Guard, I "caught" my classmate, Marvin, horsing around in the Boys Restroom and turned him in. The teacher spanked his hands--teachers could use corporal punishment, in those days—causing me and Marvin to get into a fight, after school. An adult walking down the street broke up the fight.

A couple weeks after my fight with Marvin, from my Hall Guard post, I noticed the door to the janitor's closet was open. Curious, I looked in the closet and saw a ladder attached to a wall. With no one around, I climbed the ladder all the way to the ceiling and pushed aside one of the ceiling tiles. When the sunshine poured in, I stuck my head up through the opening and realized that I was at the roof of the school.

I did not go out on to the roof that day but, two days later, I wanted to show my sister and my friend, Darrell, what I had discovered. I led them into the janitor's closet and up the ladder. I got half-way up the ladder when suddenly, the janitor burst into the closet and caught the three of us on the ladder. The janitor chewed us out and took us to Miss Beasley, Horner School's Adjustment Teacher's office.

Miss Beasley quickly fingered me as the ringleader and allowed Darrell and my sister to go to their classes. But she "read me the riot act" and told me that I was being suspended until I brought my mother to school to meet with her. When I got home and told my mother that I had been suspended, she was angrier than I had ever seen her. "Sometimes, I just don't understand you," she yelled, "You're just a poor-ass Negro like everybody else in this neighborhood." It was the only time in my life that I ever heard my mother swear.

The very next day, Mom and I went to school to meet with Miss Beasley. I listened as Miss Beasley and my mother talked about how disappointed they were with my "unsatisfactory conduct." Then, Miss Beasley sent chills down my spine when she said to my mother, "Mrs. Smith, you may want to consider sending George to another school…"

When I first heard the words, "another school," it scared me because I thought Mrs. Beasley was talking about a reform school. Then she said, "Mrs. Smith, you might want to consider sending George to a school like the University of Chicago Laboratory School, a private school that uses 'experimental' methods getting kids, like George, to work to their potential. The Lab School is expensive and most of the students there will be White. But there are some Black kids, there, too."

I had never heard of The Laboratory School, but I figured a school that had a laboratory, like in the movie Frankenstein, had to be a cool place. For the next few days, my mother and father intensely discussed whether they could afford to send me to the Lab School.

Mom repeated what Miss Beasley had said about my potential, but Dad scoffed, "What George needs is to buckle down and stop fooling around. We can't afford to send George to no Laboratory School." At that point, my mother said, "We may not be able to afford *not* to!"

In the end, my mother prevailed. I finished the semester at Horner School and applied to the Lab School. Over the Summer, I took a test, went through some interviews, and in August I was notified that I had been accepted at the

University of Chicago Laboratory School, 1953

Lab School. A few weeks later, my mother announced she had finally found an opportunity to use her shorthand as a secretary at the University of Chicago's School of Social Services Administration (SSA), which entitled our family to a **tuition rebate at the Laboratory School.**

My two best buddies on the block, Billy and Robert

My last class (fourth grade) at Henry Horner School

Me in my white suit as ring bearer at my Aunt Dorothy's wedding in 1950. My father made my suit, but I had to wear white Keds, because my mother could not find any white leather shoes that fit me. Later, I was a big hit at school because I was the first to wear sneakers to school.

—7—

"I'm Gone"
Shirley & Lee

When I was eight, a lot of the kids in my neighborhood saw me as nerdy, and when they learned that I was transferring to a special, "laboratory" school, that reinforced their perception of me. I tried to explain to my closest friends that I was "not being sufficiently challenged at Horner School and not working to my potential..." all that stuff that Miss Beasley and my mother talked about, but I could not have been very effective at explaining it because I did not understand all that stuff myself. I did not even attempt to explain that the schoolwork that I'd be doing at Lab would be "advanced," compared with the work at Horner School or that I would be entering the Lab School as a 4th grader, even though I had already completed fourth grade at Horner.

The Lab School operated on the same schedule as the college, so Lab School classes did not start until late September, weeks after Chicago's public schools were back in session, following summer vacation. So, when I finally started at Lab, my buddies were bursting to hear what it is like to go to school with White kids. I told them that there were twenty White kids in my class, many of them Jewish, and I was getting along with them just fine. My neighborhood friends never asked me about the Black kids at Lab, probably because they could not imagine that there would be any. There were five Black kids in my class, besides me.

My first few friends at Lab were White, starting with a White kid named Jim who I had met during "new student orientation" over the summer. Unfortunately, Jim and I did not remain friends for long, however. Early in the semester during a gym class, Jim pulled me into the deep water in the swimming pool, even though he knew that I could not swim. Luckily, the gym teacher, Mr. Zarvis, heard me yelling and extended a bamboo pole to me and pulled me to the side of the pool. I had swallowed so much water, I thought I was on my way to drowning. That was the end of my friendship with Jim. I did not tell my friends in the neighborhood about the swimming pool incident because I knew they would have wanted to know why I hadn't "kicked that White boy's ass." A few weeks later, however, I told my neighborhood buddies that I had learned how to swim, giving me bragging rights in the 'hood, since none of buddies knew how to swim.

One of the first things I liked about the Lab School was that we spent a lot of time in class talking about science and living things. When I mentioned the emphasis on science to my father, he said that he was not surprised and went on to explain the role the University of Chicago had played in the development of the atomic bomb and the birth of the Nuclear Age. Dad pointed out that the work had been done at Stagg Field, under the leadership of a famous physicist named Enrico Fermi…which helped explain why Fermi's daughter, Nella, was one of my teachers at the Lab School. She had taken our class on a "walking 'field trip'" across the University of Chicago campus to the West stands of Stagg Field, where her father helped develop the World's first nuclear reactor.

Besides science, the other thing that I liked about the Lab School was *Show and Tell*, which we did in class, every Monday morning. Many of my classmates, especially my White classmates, had traveled extensively to places like California, New York, Europe and even Israel and their *Show and Tell* stories were often about places they had visited. The only place I had ever been outside of Chicago was Springfield, Illinois. One day during "show and tell," I told the class about going to the Illinois State Fair in Springfield, but my classmates did not seem all that interested, since they did not ask me any questions. The next time during *Show and Tell*, I showed the class a photograph I had taken of Abraham Lincoln's house, one day, on my way to the Fairgrounds, and they were much more interested.

I had become so discouraged at not having a lot to share "show and tell" that I thought about making up a story about having taken a trip to Las Vegas. I "tested" my Las Vegas story for its "wow factor" on a White kid named Joel, while we were having lunch in the cafeteria. As soon as I mentioned Las Vegas, Joel's face lit up, "Oh, really," he exclaimed, excitedly. "What hotel did your family stay at in Vegas? When we went, we stayed at the Sands."

Suddenly trapped by my scheme, I could not recall the names of any of the Las Vegas hotels that were part of the prize packages on

TV game shows, but I could not think of any. To save face, I told Joel, that my family had stayed at The Eldorado Hotel." Joel sincerely pondered my answer, then said, "I've never heard of the Eldorado. It must not be on 'the Strip'?" "It's not!" I said.

Whew, close call!

From time to time, a young Black "teacher-in-training" named Miss Thomas was assigned to Mr. Boyd's classroom, and on one Monday, she handled *Show and Tell*. Without warning, Miss Thomas called me up to the front of the class and told me to face my classmates. I was sure that Miss Thomas had, somehow, heard that I had made up a story about having visited Las Vegas, and she was going to make me apologize to my classmates or lecture me about not being honest.

While I stood nervously in front of the class, Miss Thomas chimed, "Class, I know something about George that I'll bet the rest of you don't know. Take a good look at him. What do you think it is?" You could hear a pin drop in the classroom, with my classmates staring at me. Then, Miss Thomas announced, "Class, I happen to know that George's father made the pants that George is wearing. Aren't they beautiful? George's father is a tailor."

Some of my classmates at the Lab School in 1958. Me – middle, second row

A shaggy-haired White kid named Sam leaned over his desk and felt my trousers between his thumb and forefinger. "That's incredible!" he said, quietly. Two White girls started applauding, then the whole class erupted in applause. I felt great. And rich.

— 8 —

"My Only Love"
The Falcons

    While most of my White classmates seemed genuinely excited at the revelation that my father was a tailor, I noticed a Black girl in my class named Donna sitting with her arms folded tightly across her chest and a frown on her face. Donna always seemed to have it out for me, ever since she criticized me for having ashy skin after I had been swimming in gym class.

    "You need lotion!" she said, haughty. At first, I thought Donna was having fun with me, so I played along and teased her for having food stuck in her braces. (Donna was the first Black person I had ever seen with braces.)

    But Donna came back at me saying, "Well, at least I won't have that awful space between my teeth like you have." That's when I realized that she was not having fun with me. I had never been teased about having a "gap." A lot of people in my neighborhood had gaps. Heck, my father had a gap.

    To be honest, when I first started at the Lab School, I felt more comfortable around some of the White kids, than I did the Black kids. I wanted to be friends with some of the Black kids, but I did not know how to make that happen and none of them made a move towards me.

    Besides Donna, there was a fair-skinned Black girl named Rosemary in my class, a boy called Ronnie and a boy named Ellsworth, who the White kids called Elzie. One day, as Elzie and I passed one another in the hallway, I chirped, "Hi, Elzie!" He stopped in his tracks, leaned in close to my face and, in a voice brimming with intensity, said, "My Black friends all call me Chip or Chipper. It's short for *chip off the old block* because people say I look so much like my father. Call me Chip!" I had my first Black friend at the Lab School.

*****

In my first year at the Lab School, a couple White kids, one named Paul and one named Keith invited me to visit their homes so that we could play together on weekends. Chip, though, was the first Black kid to invite me to his home. He lived in a beautiful apartment on Hyde Park boulevard, with his father, who was a physician, and his younger brother. And Chip really did look like his father. Chip was, also, the first Black or White kid from the Lab School to visit my home at 41st and Indiana.

Lyon & Healy, the music school where I was taking trumpet lessons, formed a band comprised of kids taking music lessons on a variety of instruments. The kids' band was featured, a few times, on an after-school television program for kids on PBS and I told my friends to watch the program. The next day, following a broadcast, Chip rushed up to me and told me that he had not only seen me in the band he had also seen a friend of his named Nicky, playing tenor saxophone in the band. Chip said that Nicky attended Ray School, the public school down the street from the Lab School and the three of us should get together one day after school.

A week later, Nicky, Chip and I met after school at a nearby soda fountain. The three of us had such a good time together, we decided to start a club comprised of Black boys we knew. We named the club The Junior Gents and, between us, we added another six or seven boys who Chip and Nicky both knew. The only kid I knew who both Chip and Nicky knew was Ronnie, the other Black boy in my class at Lab, so I put Ronnie into our new club. Later, I learned that Chip and Nicky were active in a boys and girls social club called Jack and Jill club, which is how they knew so many of the same boys. Be that as it may, through Chip and Nicky, I met a whole new group of Black boys who did not go to the Lab School and were not from my neighborhood.

—9—

"Life could be a dream... life could be a dream..."
from "Sh Boom," The Chords

Unless you have lived in Chicago, chances are, you might not know that Chicago was founded by a Black man. Around 1780, Jean Baptiste Pointe DuSable, a Black man, became Chicago's first non-indigenous settler on the banks of the Chicago River. In truth, not even people who lived in Chicago knew that DuSable was Chicago's first settler, before 1933 when the Desaible Society, an organization of Black women led by my father's aunt, Annie Oliver, developed an exhibit that featured a model of the cabin in which Dusable once lived. (The name Desaible was changed to Dusable so that people would not joke that Black people were disabled.)

In my opinion, Aunt Annie should be in history books because she spearheaded the movement to have DuSable recognized. The 1933-34 World's Fair was attended by 40,000,000 visitors and by its end, the World had been exposed to the DuSable/Chicago story.

Even though Aunt Annie's efforts helped bring DuSable's significance to light as founder of Chicago, when I was a kid, there were surprisingly few things in the city of Chicago named for DuSable. However, one place that was named for DuSable was the all-Black, DuSable Public High School at 49th and Wabash on the Southside, which was a mile from my house.

DuSable High School was a mainstay for thousands of Black people living in Bronzeville, and among its alums are some of the most accomplished Black people in history, including jazz greats and entertainers like Gene Ammons, Nat "King" Cole, Dinah Washington, comedian Redd Foxx, Soul Train's, Don Cornelius and business icons John Johnson, the founder of Johnson Publishing Company, the publisher of Ebony and Jet Magazines, and Chicago's first Black mayor, Harold Washington.

In the Spring of 1954, as DuSable high school prepared to play for the Illinois State Championship in Boys Basketball and folks in my neighborhood went bonkers. The 1954 DuSable team had won 31 straight games and, entering the Championship game, was not only the first Chicago Public school to reach the Illinois State Championship game and, perhaps more significantly, DuSable High School was about to become the first all-Black school with a Black coach to win an "open" (non-segregated) State Championship, in America, in any sport.

The 1954 DuSable Panthers were a trendsetter in high school basketball with their knee-high, pro-style socks and free-wheeling, high-flying style of play. Dusable even featured a team of dancing cheerleaders. One of the stars of the '54 DuSable team, Paxton Lumpkin, was such a gifted ball-handler, he went on to replace the legendary Marquis Haynes as the featured ballhandler of the world-famous, Harlem Globetrotters. DuSable even warmed up to "Sweet Georgia Brown," like the Globetrotters.

DuSable's opponent in the State Championship game was Mount Vernon, a small, mostly White, "downstate Illinois" town, nearly 300 miles from Chicago. On the night of the game, my father and I went to his brother's house to watch the game on TV. Uncle Johnny was a widower with seven children, ranging in age from seven to 17. I was especially eager to watch the game on TV with my cousins.

Before the game started, my cousin Allen foretold, "DuSable won't win the game if it is close 'cause white folks ain't gonna let no Black, 'city slickers' from Chicago, win a close game." I had heard my father express similar sentiments, many times, when we watched boxing matches between a Black boxer and a White boxer He would say, "A Black boxer has got to either cut a White boxer until he bleeds real bad, or he has to knock him out because them ol' white judges ain't gonna let a Black fighter win 'on points.'" It was another early lesson I learned about race: if an outcome is subjective, Black people won't win.

From the start of the DuSable-Mount Vernon game, most of the referee's calls seemed to go against DuSable. Mount Vernon had one Black player on its team, but his presence was not enough to balance the scales. At one point during the game, DuSable scored eight, straight points, only to have each one of those points taken off the scoreboard by a questionable referee's call. In the end, DuSable lost the game by six points. I was only nine years old in the spring of 1954 and, watching those White referees "steal" that game from DuSable was the most traumatic experience of my young life. As I tried to fight back tears, my father said, "Ain't no sense in cryin.' Get used to it. That's the way they do Black people!" It might have been the first time I ever heard that expression.

Weeks after that game, a lot of folks, including a surprising number of Black people in my neighborhood, convinced themselves that the DuSable kids had not played well enough to win and complained that blaming DuSable's loss on the White referees, was something they called "playing the race card." Those people, and some White, Chicago sports writers, argued that DuSable had lost to a "mentally tougher, more disciplined team" in Mount Vernon. For me, the assessment of DuSable's performance in that Championship game marked the first time I heard a theme that I still hear to this day: Black athletes are more physically gifted than their White opponents, but Whites are smarter, play harder and are more disciplined. (What a crock!)

It was not until the '70s, that it came to light that gambling interests may have had something to do with the outcome of that DuSable-Mount Vernon game. A White journalist named Ira Berkow documented that and one of the referees who officiated that DuSable-Mount Vernon game was later indicted for "fixing" high school basketball games" and known to use racial slurs while officiating games. Just sayin'...

About a year after the DuSable basketball debacle, in August 1955, I was visiting my relatives in Springfield, Illinois, when I first heard about the murder of Emmett Till, the Black, fourteen years old Chicago boy who had been abducted and murdered for allegedly "whistling" at a White woman in a small town in Mississippi. The media in Springfield did not cover the story all that much, but when I called home and spoke with my parents, I learned that Till had "made a pass" at a White woman and how White men took Till from his grandfather's house, at night, and killed him. My father warned me that "Negroes have to be careful how they act, around White people."

Coming back to Chicago from Springfield, my parents picked up my sister and me at the Illinois Central train station at Roosevelt Road and Michigan Avenue then drove down State Street towards our home at 41st and Indiana. When we crossed 39th and State Street, we encountered hundreds, if not thousands, of Black people in the street, forcing traffic to slow to a crawl. Finally, my father was forced to stop in front of Roberts Temple Church of God in Christ, between 40th and 41st State Street. Thousands of people had lined up outside Roberts Temple there to view the bloated and mutilated body of Emmett Till.

Among my neighborhood buddies, the question was whether our parents would take us to Roberts Temple to view Emmett Till's body. My friend Billy's mother was willing to take some of kids in the neighborhood to view Till, but my parents objected to the voyeurism they associated with viewing Till's body and would not give me permission to go with Billy and his mother. Based on what Billy later described, I tried to imagine what Till's remains must have looked like but, I must admit, I was not prepared for the photo of Till's body that I finally saw in *Jet* Magazine. It was horrific and haunting.

*****

By the time I turned 13, the litany of racial incidents occurring in my lifetime included the Harvey Clark/Cicero, Illinois incident in1951; Rosa Parks and the Montgomery (AL) Bus Boycott, led by a young, Black preacher named Martin Luther King, Jr. in 1954; DuSable's loss and, finally, the lynching of Emmett Till in 1955. But it was DuSable's loss in 1954 that most made me aware of racism.

—10—

"Did You See Jackie Robinson Hit That Ball?"
Buddy Johnson

Although she was barely out of high school, Frances attracted more attention than of any other women in my neighborhood. She was slender and shapely, with swarthy skin and silky, black hair and, when she walked down the street, everybody would turn and watch. I noticed that the men in the neighborhood called her "fine," but the ladies called her "fast." What really set Francis apart, however, was not the way she looked; it was how well she could play 16" softball. She was the only woman in the neighborhood who played softball with the men.

Growing up in the '50s, softball and/or baseball were the most popular sports in my neighborhood, more popular, even, than basketball. There had been a long tradition of baseball in the Black community, even before Jackie Robinson broke Major League Baseball's "color line" in 1947. Negro Leagues teams like the Chicago Brown Bombers and the Chicago American Giants were hugely popular in the Black community. In fact, one of my father's regular customers was Elwood "Bingo" DeMoss, a former Negro League player and manager of the Chicago Brown Bombers and Chicago American Giants. Mr. DeMoss lived in the 40th block on Indiana Avenue and whenever I would deliver his cleaning to him, I could always count on Mr. DeMoss to give me a nice tip and tell me stories about the heyday of the Negro Leagues, while showing me newspaper clippings. The Negro Leagues played an All-Star game every summer at Southside Park (which became Comiskey Park) where the Major League Chicago White Sox played and, whenever the Negro League were playing, hundreds of Black people would stream past my house, going towards 35th Street.

Thanks to my neighbor, Elwood "Bingo" DeMoss and the Negro Leagues and the emergence of Jackie Robinson, baseball was the most popular sport in my neighborhood, when I was a boy.

I got into baseball when I was 12. I did not fully appreciate the significance of Jackie Robinson, I suppose, because, by 1956, most Major League teams had at least one Black player. The Chicago Cubs were my favorite Major League team and Cubs' star Ernie Banks, who was Black, was one of my favorite players.

One day, I casually mentioned to my father that Mickey Mantle, the New York Yankee's White superstar, was another one of my favorite players but my father admonished me, saying, "A Black boy should have Black heroes!" It was a reminder that race is always important to somebody. It was not until I was much older that I realized that my father Dad saw Jackie Robinson as a hero for more than his prowess as a baseball player but also because he admired the way Robinson was a fighter for racial justice in and outside of baseball.

Jackie Robinson and my father nearly crossed paths during WWII

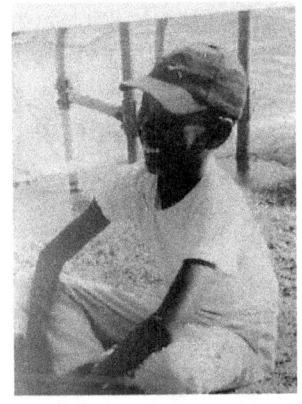

In 1955, when I told my father that I wanted to be a Major League baseball player he told me that I was too skinny. Wonder what gave him that idea?

because they both spent time in Hawaii. Their respective Hawaii experiences were very different, however: Before entering the Army, Robinson was in Hawaii playing semi-professional football on a racially integrated team. A year or so later, my father was in the segregated Navy in Hawaii. A short time after returning to California from playing football in Hawaii, Robinson got drafted into the Army. He was commissioned as a Second Lieutenant and assigned to an all-Black Tank unit, the 761st Black Panthers, in Fort Hood, Texas.

At Fort Hood, Robinson got embroiled in a situation that resulted in his being court-martialed. While riding an Army bus at Fort Hood, Robinson sat next to a light skin, Black woman in the middle of the bus. The White bus driver thought the woman sitting next to Robinson was White, so he pulled the bus over and ordered Robinson to move to the back of the bus, as was then-required under Texas law. An argument ensued and Robinson refused to move to the back of the bus. The bus driver called the MPs, and Robinson was arrested and charged. Robinson was court-martialed in August 1944 and then was acquitted and honorably discharged from the Army in November. As you might expect, stories about Robinson's fight against the discrimination directed at Black servicemen came to light around the same time as he was "breaking the color line" in Major League Baseball and Black people, my father included, identified as much with Robinson's struggles in a segregated United States military, as they did Robinson's exploits in baseball. By the 1950s, it was impossible to separate "race" from sports in the U.S.

One Sunday evening, in the summer of 1956, when I was 12, my father took the family to the drive-in. The drive-in had a "kiddie land" playground at the base of the screen, where kids could play until it got dark enough to show the movie. The playground had "batting cages," where you could put a quarter in and then try to bat balls rifled from a pitching machine. Since it was still too light outside to show movies, I walked to the batting cages.

When I got to the cages, there was no one else around. I picked out a bat and inserted my quarter into the "pitching machine," which lit up and began to hum and spit out pitches. After I swung at a few pitches, three boisterous White men barged into my batting cage, each one swinging a bat. The men forced me to duck and get out of the way. Suddenly I heard my father yelling, "Leave that boy alone!" Dad was running towards the batting cage, brandishing a golf club. The three White men dropped the bats they had been swinging and ran out of the cage, disappearing into the parking lot.

After checking to see if I was okay, my father told me to "go ahead and finish batting," while he stood guard. But, as soon as I "got back into the batting cage, the pitching machine whirred to a stop. As my father and I walked back to the car, he fussed at me. "Boy, you've got to be more careful. I tell you that all the time. You've got watch White people. They're not all like those White people you go to school with at the Laboratory School. Some White people will kill you. They don't care if you're a kid or not." In the wake of the murder of Emmett Till, my father had made his point.

Crowds viewing Emmett Till's body at Robert's Temple Church of God in Christ, two blocks from my house, in 1955. I was 11.

My father's Aunt Annie Oliver seated in front of the De'Saible (DuSable) Society which she headed and the exhibit of DuSable's cabin at 1933 World's Fair in Chicago. DuSable, a Black man, "founded" Chicago's in 1779.

The 1954 DuSable High School basketball team whose controversial loss in the Illinois State Basketball Championship game that I witnessed on TV. The game was my most painful "race" moment. I was 10.

—11—

"Why Do You Have to Go?"
The Dells

During the summer of 1957, prior to my starting high school, my sister and I visited my father's sister, Aunt Ann, her physician husband, Uncle Jack, and their two sons, George Frazier, who was 19, and MacDonald who was 15. Two other cousins from Chicago, Johnny and Marie, were already in LA, living with Aunt Ann and Uncle Jack.

I was excited about going to California, even though I regretted not having had the trip to talk about, back when I was in "show and tell" in 4th grade. The train ride on the Santa Fe El Capitan to California took two days and I was thrilled as the Western landscape that I grew up watching in "cowboy movies" rolled past.

Besides seeing the amazing sites of Southern California, including Hollywood (Unfortunately, we never got to Disneyland during my visit to Los Angeles.) I got to see a few "stars," including Little Richard, who lived up the street from my aunt. And, actor Johnny Lee, who played the character "Calhoun" in the "Amos and Andy" television show, went to the same church as my aunt and uncle. The other big takeaway from my trip to Los Angeles was that my aunt served me grits for breakfast, one morning. I had never had grits before (my mother never fixed grits) so I did not know how to eat them. To me, grits looked like Cream of Wheat, so I tried putting sugar and milk on the grits, getting a good laugh out my cousins as they watched me in disbelief, struggling with grits.

*****

Things really started to change in 1957. High school at Lab did not seem to be as carefree or fun as it had once been. One cause of a change happened after the Soviet Union successfully launched Sputnik 1, the first artificial Earth satellite, during the fall of my freshman year. The University of Chicago had always put a major emphasis on science, but with the launching of Sputnik 1, America feared that the U.S. had fallen dangerously behind the Soviet Union in science and technology, and high schools felt pressure to get more serious about those two subjects. The change made me feel mature, like I was contributing to the betterment of society.

Making the freshman baseball team at University High (U-High), the Lab school's high school, felt good too. Among my friends, both at school and in the neighborhood, playing sports was a big deal. I remember standing around with a group of my friends and taking turns bragging about the sports we were playing. A couple of guys played basketball, and others were on the football team.

When it came around to Scrappy, he smiled and boasted, "Biology Club!" Scrappy had never shown much interest in playing sports, and we all laughed. But the more I thought about it, the more I was impressed that Scrappy was not ashamed to admit that he valued the Biology Club over a sport. Scrappy, by the way, became a physician, while none of the rest of us became professional athletes.

My father's cleaning and tailoring business was also undergoing changes. He found that he could no longer count on the revenue from making as many as 25 suits a year for men and women, so he had to change his business plan. "Everybody is dressing more casual than they used to these days," he quipped, "plus the men in this neighborhood aren't going to church much, so they don't need suits," he laughed. "And they are not hiring Negroes in those management jobs in those downtown offices. There is not much of a market for tailor-made suits around here."

Dad countered the decline in demand for tailoring by adding consignment sales to the business, capitalizing on the many contacts he had established over the years with well-dressed clients, including White clients he had cultivated back when he tailored at a Jewish-owned shop on the North Side. Consignment sales really took off, giving the business the shot in the arm it needed.

As business picked up, Dad scheduled me to work more hours. Besides cleaning up and taking care of our dog, who "guarded" the shop, the most important job I performed was waiting on customers, which freed Dad to be able to go around the city, collecting clothes for resale. Once I started working in the shop after coming from school every day and all day on Saturdays, I no longer received an allowance from my parents while earning a weekly salary of two dollars. Bus fare was only thirteen cents, so I was in good financial shape. During the winter months, I did not mind having to work in the shop, but as the weather warmed up in the spring, I was eager to play baseball, but working from eight in the morning until eight at night on Saturdays did not leave much time for baseball.

My childhood was over.

—12—

"Whispering Bells"
Del-Vikings

As of June 1958, I had been attending the Lab School for five years, from 4th grade through my freshman year of high school. Overall, I was satisfied with how I was doing, academically and, with Chip "coaching" me, I had begun to shed some of my awkwardness when it came to talking to pretty, Black girls. I was looking forward to sophomore year at U High but, in the middle of the summer, I got some startling news from my parents: we were moving from 41st and Indiana to Lake Meadows, a high-rise apartment complex, a block from the lake shore.

Lake Meadows was promoted as "Chicago's venture into integrated urban living," meaning there would be Black and White people living there. Compared to the old, dilapidated, two-story walk-up where we had lived with three other families on 41st and Indiana, Lake Meadows was a step-up, with its 22-story, high rise buildings that, from a distance, appeared to be made of glass. My parents had managed to buy the building on 41st Street and were collecting rent from two families.

Then came the real stunner: after learning that we were moving to Lake Meadows, my parents told me that I would be leaving the Lab School and going back into public school because they could not afford the rent at Lake Meadows and the tuition at the Lab School. I was excited about moving to Lake Meadows, but I was not sure how I felt about having to go back to public school. The public high schools in Lake Meadows' district were Wendell Phillips and Dunbar Vocational, both all-Black schools. After five years of going to a school that was 90% White, I worried about how I would adapt and fit in at an all-Black school.

At 41st and Indiana, I lived in DuSable High School's district. However, Wendell Phillips High School was a few blocks away on 39th Street, so I was familiar with some of the thuggish kids who attended Phillips, and I wanted no part of that kind of environment.

I wondered if I could go to school in peace and get a good education at an all-Black school or if I would have to fight my way home every day and worry about somebody trying to take my lunch money... or steal my coat. Rather, I felt that I would be more comfortable in a racially integrated public school.

There was one integrated high school near Lake Meadows, DeLaSalle Catholic High School, which was also an all-boys school. When I brought up the possibility of attending DeLaSalle, my father told me that he had no intention of paying tuition again. "Besides," he said, "all that Catholic hocus pocus ain't got nothin to do with Negroes."

My father's position on integrated schools was confusing because, while he often complained about the disadvantages that Black kids face in America as a result of attending under-funded, all-Black public schools, at other times he said "going to school with White kids was overrated," pointing out how many, "successful Negroes like Dempsey Travis (realtor),and John Johnson (publisher of *Ebony, Jet* and *Tan* magazines)" were products of all-Black, Chicago public high schools.

My mother was empathetic with my preference to go to an integrated school. "One thing you can count on," she would say, "is that White people are going to make sure their children get what they need from a high school to prepare them for college." My mother also seemed to understand the anxiety I felt about being able to fit-in at an all-Black, public school so she set about trying to find an integrated, public high school that I could attend by using someone else's home address.

Although Chicago required that kids attend the public schools in their district, using a friend or relative's address to attend a particular school was not uncommon. My first choice for a public high school was Hyde Park, which was not far from the Lab School. In fact, my buddy Nicky was at Hyde Park. But my family did not know anyone who lived in Hyde Park's district whose address I could use. Hirsch High School was my second choice, but again my family did not know anyone whose address I could use to attend Hirsch.

One Sunday, my mother happened to see an article in the paper about a newly-built, Chicago public high school at 96th and Michigan, in one of the few integrated communities in Chicago, called Roseland. Harlan High School was named for Associate Supreme Court Justice, John Marshall Harlan, who, despite descending from a slave-owning family, was the lone dissenting vote in the landmark, 1896 case of Plessy v. Ferguson, arguing that "segregation based on race was unconstitutional." Harlan High School was being touted as "an experiment in integration," an appropriate commemoration for Justice Harlan, I suppose.

I don't know how much my mother knew about the history of John Marshall Harlan, but she recognized from what was being written about the new high school that Harlan might turn out to be the kind of integrated public high school setting where I might be okay, and when an old friend of hers who lived in Harlan's district said that I could use her address, Harlan would be my high school, eight miles from Lake Meadows. My mother's friend's last name just happened to be Smith, by the way.

In my last year at the Lab School, my closest friends were all Black, and a funny thing happened when I told them that I was leaving Lab: I learned that most of them were leaving Lab too. Chip was heading to a military academy in New York, Ronnie was going to Hirsch, and Jim Pitts, who 6'8," was a young basketball star and was transferring to Marshall High School on the West Side, which was a Chicago high school basketball powerhouse. Only two of the seven Black boys in my class stayed at Lab beyond freshman year, but I never learned why so many Black males left Lab while most of the Black girls stayed.

—13—

"It's All in the Game"
Tommy Edwards

In 1953, Lake Meadows was considered an "urban redevelopment project," transforming former all-Black, slum neighborhoods, comprised of rotting, nineteenth-century mansions and buildings, into good-looking apartment buildings. intended to attract the White and Black "middle class." Lake Meadows started out with five, twelve-story apartment buildings, from 35th to 33rd, and east of South Park. By 1958, however, Lake Meadows had added four 22-story high-rise apartment buildings with balconies, from 33rd to 32nd Street. My family moved into a three-bedroom apartment on the fifteenth floor of 501 East 32nd Street, in what, at the time, was the newest of those 22-story buildings.

To me, Lake Meadows was remarkable. From our balcony, I could see what seemed like the entire Southside of Chicago, as well as the Lake. And right in the middle of the complex of high-rise apartment buildings was an open field of lush grass, where I noticed Black and White kids, playing baseball. I was so eager to play on that grass that on my first Sunday in Lake Meadows, I put on my baseball cap, tucked my baseball glove under my arm and headed for that field.

On the way down, the elevator stopped on the eleventh floor, and a Black teenager with a baseball glove and a cap cocked on the back of his head got on the elevator. When he saw my glove he grinned, stuck-out his hand and said, "Hi, my name is David. C'mon, I'll show you where we play!" David and I walked to the field where Black and White kids were playing baseball. David led me over to a group of Black teenagers who were sitting in the grass, waiting for the next game, and began introducing me.

Right away, I was surprised to see faces I recognized, including a guy who had just graduated from U-High, Bill McClaskey, and a guy named Norman Loftis, who I knew from 41st Street, where we called him "Mr. All Star" because he was always outfitted in gear for whatever sport we were playing in the schoolyard.

All the guys I met that day were bright, funny and engaging. I could not have asked for a better welcome into Lake Meadows. Perhaps the most amazing coincidence was that most of my new friends were in high school at either Phillips or Dunbar, reminding me that I might need to rethink my bias against all-Black public schools. As a kid called Zip shook my hand, his eyes drifted up to my cap and he quipped, "Man, you look like 'Elmer Fudd' in that cap!" sparking laughter from everyone there. My closest friends still call me Fudd, to this day.

Despite having to do some serious soul searching because I felt so comfortable around the "brothers" I just met in Lake Meadows, I was still not ready to throw caution to the wind and go to Phillips or Dunbar. Instead, I with the plan to go to Harlan. I was 14.

—14—

"Tears On My Pillow"
Little Anthony and the Imperials

When Harlan opened in the Fall of 1958, I was a nervous wreck, worried that school authorities would learn that I was not living in Harlan's district. As I went back and forth to school, using public transportation on busses and the "L," I worried that someone would see me. In fact, early in the semester, a girl in my class named Elaine told me that she noticed me catching a CTA (Chicago Transit Authority) bus after school and asked me where I lived. I told her I caught the bus after school on my way to my father's tailor shop, where I worked. Elaine pressed me about my address and when I gave her my "Harlan address," she looked at me skeptically, and said, "That's around the corner from where I live. Funny, I ain't never seen you in the neighborhood." I just shrugged.

Black families in Chicago were willing to take chances on their kids getting caught for going to schools outside their district, rather than settling for their kids going to neighborhood schools they believed were inferior. As I caught the southbound CTA bus each morning on my way to school, I began to see more and more Black kids, heading to Harlan, including a girl in my homeroom named Dorothy. One morning, Dorothy and I talked about what excuse we should use if ever the bus we were on ever got caught in a traffic jam, causing us to be late to school. Black families valued integrated schools because they improved the likelihood that their children would get a decent education. For the record though, I have always wondered how many White families valued integrated schools.

When Harlan first opened, it was about 50% White and 50% Black. The Roseland community was going through racial change, meaning that Blacks were moving in as Whites were moving out. In Chicago, when neighborhoods underwent racial change, it seemed to happen fast. One year, a neighborhood might be 10% Black and 90% White, and the next year it might be 50/50, while the year after that, the numbers could be 90% Black and 10% White. Racially changing neighborhoods were often a source of racial tension, and a month into my first semester at Harlan, I found myself in a potentially volatile racial situation.

Following gym class, as I was in the locker room, about to shower, a White kid I did not know plopped down next to me and began working the combination to his locker. The White kid nodded "hello" and I nodded back. A slight movement caught my eye, causing me to stop and look around as the White kid continued working his combination. That is when I saw Lewis, a Black kid in street clothes, lying on his stomach on top of a bank of lockers, watching the White kid work his combination. When Lewis realized that I saw him, he held his finger up to his lips, signaling me not to say anything. By that time, the White kid had opened his locker, tossed in his gym clothes, relocked it and headed off to the shower.

Lewis, swung his legs around, let them dangle for a second, then dropped down next to me on the bench. Without saying anything, he proceeded to work the White kid's combination lock, as if it was his own. I watched Lewis for a few seconds, then exclaimed in disbelief, "Lewis, man, I know you're not about to steal stuff from that White dude's locker!" My rebuke did not slow Lewis down, and without making eye contact, he thrust his arm into the White kid's locker and snapped, "Man, these White boys got shit you and me ain't got!"

After groping around inside, Lewis abruptly jerked his arm out of the locker, sniffed his fingertips and grimaced. I figured he must have touched the White kid's sweaty shorts or jock strap. Lewis stuck his arm back inside the locker then stood up, slapped at the White kid's locker door and griped, "Ain't shit in this mutha fucka!"

He hitched at his belt, as if regaining his dignity, and strutted out of the locker room, empty-handed, leaving the White kid's locker partially open. Seconds later, the White kid came back from the shower, his hair still dripping wet. He saw his locker door open and muttered, "Damn, I thought I closed my locker!"

Since I had not seen Lewis take anything out of the locker and since I did not want to escalate the situation into a racial incident unnecessarily, I picked up on the White kid's remark that he thought he had closed his locker. "Yeah, man," I said, "you gotta watch stuff like that." Then, I re-locked my own locker and went to the shower. When I got back from the shower, the White kid was almost fully dressed. Since I could not be sure if Lewis had ever watched me work my combination, I planned to change my lock, and I told the White kid that he might want to do the same thing. He agreed.

Later, I thought about what might have happened if I had told the White kid about Lewis breaking into his locker. I imagined a group of White vigilantes coming to lynch Lewis, or worse— a group of angry Blacks kids coming after me for having snitched on Lewis. Either way, race would have been the cause of the conflict. Recalling Lewis excuse for opening the locker, I thought about pulling him aside to discredit the myth that all White people are better off than all Black people, but I decided I would let it go. Having spent time around some very affluent Black people, I knew that there were Black people who had more "shit" than some White people. In fact, the more I thought about it, the more I figured that the White kid who Lewis had tried to steal from might have had less than Lewis. After all, a White kid who really *did* have "shit that you and me ain't got" would likely be attending a high school in an all-White suburb, not an inner-city public school in a racially changing neighborhood.

Other than the situation involving Lewis, I never encountered any racial situations at Harlan. I think it was because the White and Black kids in my sophomore class had been freshmen together at other high school in the area. So for most of the students who, like me, had entered Harlan as sophomores, Harlan was not their first experience in an integrated school. I had White and Black friends at Harlan.

Harlan offered standard high school curricula, including social studies, math, science and a language. I took three years of Latin. Every one of my classes was integrated so that every student, Black or White, had comparable learning experiences in school. Harlan had very few Hispanic students. Being a new school, Harlan did not offer much in the way of extracurricular activities. There were varsity boys basketball and cross-country teams, language clubs and a debate team.

The lack of extracurricular activities was not an issue for me because I did not have much time for activities anyway, since I had to work in the shop every day after school and on weekends. One Saturday, I was able to talk my father into giving me time-off from work to get together with Nicky and some other guys to try and start a "rock and roll/R&B garage band." After only one attempt at a rehearsal, however, the band "crashed and burned" after the guy who let us use his garage for practice found his father's old porn movies in a box. He stopped the rehearsal to search the garage for a movie projector.

Being able to hang out with classmates after school might have helped me socially, but I enjoyed my years at Harlan High School overall.

—15—

"Will You Still Love Me Tomorrow"
The Shirelles

Being able to socialize with the kids at Harlan outside of school would have especially helped me in my relationships with girls. But Harlan was so far away from Lake Meadows, so it was hard for me to date any girls from Harlan. I did not have a car and Lake Meadows was too far from Roseland to travel to and from on public transportation at night. There were girls at Harlan who I thought about asking out, but I settled for just calling them on the phone.

At the start of my senior year, I began to think about just who I might ask to my Senior Prom. There was a White girl who I liked at Harlan named Diana, who I knew liked me, but neither she nor I ever talked about the dynamics of being an "interracial couple." I was not inclined to find out how a racially changing neighborhood like Roseland would react to seeing an interracial couple at a bus stop at night. There were also a couple Black girls who I liked at Harlan, but one of them got pregnant and transferred to another school and the other one, Alice, mysteriously disappeared and left Harlan at the end of our junior year (more about Alice, later.).

In the summer of 1960, Diane, a girl I had known for a long time, moved into my building in Lake Meadows. Diane was Nicky's cousin and had also "gone with" another friend of mine's older brother, who was a college student. Both Diane and I happened to be taking summer school classes at Hyde Park, so I discovered she had moved into my building one day when we rode the same bus on the way home. Diane lived on the seventeenth floor, and by fall I was regularly running up the two flights of stairs to Diane's apartment to visit. By winter, Diane and I were dating.

One cold night in January, Diane and I were in a jitney cab, coming from a stage show at the Regal Theater, where the popular group, The Shirelles, had performed. Diane was riding along, looking out the window of the taxi as I chatted with another passenger in the taxi who was also coming from the Regal. Diane suddenly interrupted and asked, "Hey, Fudd, what color tuxedo are you wearing to the prom?" And just like that, I knew who my prom date would be. I was on *cloud nine*!

I imagined driving to the prom in my father's car, with Diane seated next to me. With my "learner's permit," I had begun driving my father and myself home from the shop every night. Dad told me he was "comfortable" with my driving, and in March he encouraged me to "go ahead and get a driver's license." We drove to the Division of Motor Vehicles, where I passed the test and got my driver's license.

Later I asked Dad if I could use the car to go on a date, but he told me, "No…I need the car for business. I can't afford to have anything happen to the car in an accident." I decided not to press the matter for the time being and was satisfied driving home from the shop. The prom was not until May. Several of my friends were driving their parents' cars, but I did not want to keep asking my father and use up my "asks" before I even got to May. After bringing home excellent grades for the "marking period" in March, I decided it was a good time to finalize my plans for Prom night and the car one night over dinner.

When I asked Dad if he would consider closing the shop a little early on my Prom night so that I would have enough time to drive him and me home from the shop, freshen up, change into my tux, run upstairs to pick up Diane and head to the prom, he stopped chewing long enough to ask, "What car are you driving? You know you can't drive my car. I need my car for business." Then he resumed chewing. I was devastated. The next day when I told my buddy PJ that my father was not going to let me use the car to drive to the prom, he said, "Aww, that's no problem, we can double-date." And we did.

—16—

"For many years I was the glory of Chicago's Southside
I lived the life of the hip, Thrilling to Coltrane's saxophone And spoke a coded language Only the hip could understand"
"Delirium" by Norman Loftis

In June 1961, a week before graduating from high school, me, Norman and four other guys were playing basketball on the lighted outdoor basketball courts at Pershing Elementary School in Lake Meadows. When the game ended, Norman invited all of us to his apartment to "cool off... and order pizza." Norman told us that his mother was at work, so we would have the apartment to ourselves. We all said, "Yeah!"

We straggled into Norman's apartment, plopping our sweaty bodies down, sticking to the plastic covered furniture. When Norman went into the kitchen to make Kool Aid and order pizza, one of the guys, Sykes, turned on the stereo and tuned it to a popular, Black radio station. Norman immediately exploded out of the kitchen, waving his finger like Dikembe Mutombo and taunting, "No, no, no... Y'all gonna listen to some real music tonight," and with that warning, Norman switched the stereo from "radio" mode to "phonograph," pulled four Miles Davis albums from a cabinet, took the records out of the sleeves and "stacked" the records on the spindle, looked at us and smiled, smugly, as he pressed the "play" button, then strutted back into the kitchen. A guy we called Sonny leaned over and whispered to me, "Fudd, man, we 'finna pay a high-ass price for some 'God damn Kool-Aid.'"

Norman, like a lot of Black guys his age, seemed obsessed with passing himself off as "cooler" than anybody else, in the way he walked, the way he talked and with his taste in music. It wasn't enough to be a slick dancer and to be up on the latest R&B and rock and roll recordings that you could hear on the radio. If you were "cool," you let people know you were "into jazz" and preferred listening to Thelonious Monk or John Coltrane or Miles Davis. Davis was an especially popular choice among young brothers like Norman, because Davis projected a "cool" mystique in the way that he carried himself and in the way that he looked, a dark-skinned, stylishly dressed, Black musician who eschewed the traditional brassy sound of the trumpet, in exchange for the sound of the Harmon mute. Everything about Davis was different, sophisticated and cool, including his music. A lot of Black people like my friend Sonny did not like Davis's "strange sounding" music and saw Davis's "cool" persona as arrogance.

The music that changed me

Despite being a trumpet player myself, I was not familiar with much of Miles Davis's music. One time, when I was still at the Lab School, I attended a jazz festival with Chip and his father where Davis's band performed. Except for a tune called *All Blues*, I did not get much out of the band's performance or Davis's playing. What did make a strong impression on me was the way he and his band just laid their horns down on the stage and walked off at the end of the set, without so much as a bow or wave to the audience. Some people in the crowd booed. So that night at Norman's, I would have been content listening to the R&B being played on that Black radio station.

As soon as the Davis records started playing, everybody in the room began complaining. The complaining got so loud that Norman came out of the kitchen and rejected the record that was playing. A couple of times. Norman had played parts of *Sketches of Spain*, *Porgy and Bess* and *Kind of Blue*, and we rejected all of it. Some of the guys delighted in tormenting poor Norman. He finally came out of the kitchen with a pitcher of Grape Kool-Aid and slammed the pitcher down with such force that some of the Kool-Aid spilled out over the top. He grumbled, "Y'all niggas are pitiful. Black people need to broaden the music they listen to!"

Sulking, Norman sat in a chair in the foyer, away from the rest of us. At that moment, the last Miles Davis record on the spindle dropped to the platter. With everyone talking and complaining, I could barely hear the music. I did not want the other guys to know that I liked what I was hearing from bass player Paul Chamber's intro to the lyrical, melodic fills of pianist Wynton Kelly.

When Davis began stating the melody of the tune through his Harmon mute, I recognized the tune as *Some Day My Prince Will Come*, a song I first heard in a Walt Disney movie called *Snow White and the Seven Dwarfs*, when I was a little boy. My mother got the sheet music and played it on our piano at home. With everybody else hissing and complaining, I leaned in closer to the nearest speaker to hear better. Yet a few bars into the tune, Norman had heard enough of the griping in the room and stopped the record. He put his albums back into the cabinet and left the room, choosing to wait for the pizza from the kitchen. With Norman out of the room, Sykes switched back to the R&B radio station.

Later that night as I was walking home from Norman's, I kept hearing the opening bars to *Some Day My Prince Will Come*, and I looked forward to listening to the whole tune one day.

Norman's ego never diminished. (I once saw Norman admiring his own reflection in the door of a freshly washed car.) Norman asked me if I wanted to hear a poem he had written. I did not like listening to poetry, but I was willing to listen to the poem he had written. Once he started reading his poem, I tried to *hear* whatever it was that he was trying to *say*, but after I heard him use the word *phantasmagorical* in his poem, I tuned him out. I felt that Norman was trying to show off.

—17—

"Let's Go, Let's Go, Let's Go"
Hank Ballard & The Midnighters

When I graduated high school, I had no idea what to do about college. In fact, I was ashamed of myself on graduation night when I heard how many of my Black classmates had solid plans for college. Guys who I had been goofing around with for three years surprised me when I learned that they had been taking care of business and getting themselves admitted into college. For example, Tom Davis, a Black kid with whom I shared a lot of laughs, was deciding whether to attend The United States Military Academy at West Point or Stanford. Tom?

All during my senior year of high school, my mother kept talking about college, as did my counselors at school. Yet despite taking all college-prep classes, I still was not focused on college. And whenever I started to investigate potential colleges, I got bogged down in the arduous task of sorting through options, including the complexities of financial aid— reminding me of how much time I had wasted. Instead of studying harder to get better grades and qualifying for financial aid (including earning a music scholarship and fulfilling my mother's dream of having me play in a college marching band) I was too distracted to buckle down. In short, I did not have a clue as to how to proceed.

One of my friends in Lake Meadows was a brother named Gilbert Brown. He and I coached a "Pony League" baseball team of fourteen-year-old boys living in and around Lake Meadows, and we became good friends. Gilbert had graduated from Phillip High School a semester before me and had completed a semester at the University of Illinois at Navy Pier in Chicago. When I told Gilbert that I was having trouble deciding where and how to get into college, he suggested that I consider The Pier because "it is a good school and affordable," and he offered to guide me through the process.

Before the University of Illinois at Chicago Circle Campus was opened in 1965, students at the University of Illinois in Chicago were expected to complete two years at The Pier, then transfer to the main University of Illinois campus in downstate Champaign (about 135 miles from Chicago) to graduate. I knew my parents could not afford any of the local, private, four-year colleges such as Loyola, DePaul or Roosevelt, and I did not want to go to a teacher's college or a junior college, so I took Gilbert's advice and applied to The Pier. I got accepted and with Gilbert and my friend Billy Adams's help, I got enrolled as a Liberal Arts student.

The University of Illinois at Navy Pier

When I told my father that I had been accepted at the University of Illinois at Navy Pier he remained skeptical. He told me that he never doubted that I had "the intelligence for college," he just questioned my maturity and whether I would "stick with it long enough to do what is necessary to get it done." My inability to stick with things until they are done was a recurring criticism directed at me, but at least I was going to college.

The Navy Pier campus was a real, fully operating pier for loading and unloading container ships and tankers, and it extended nearly a mile out into Lake Michigan. Part of the Pier's interior warehousing space was converted into classrooms, lecture halls and laboratories and accommodated a couple thousand college students. Although the Pier was an unspectacularly proletariat structure that you entered from the craggy, Lake Michigan shoreline, it was fully accredited, and with its rigorous academic reputation, was known as "Oxford on the Rocks."

Somehow, between Gilbert and Adams, I ended up taking five classes: World History, Biology (Lecture and Laboratory), Rhetoric 101 and German. I do not remember why I took German. Adams was taking Spanish and Gilbert was taking French, but it did not take me long to find out that taking German was a big mistake. I struggled with German from the start, and to make matters worse, I discovered that my German teacher lived in my building in Lake Meadows, an unanticipated hazard of living in an integrated community. When I bumped into her in the elevator of the building, she grinned broadly as we greeted each other in German, which frankly was the extent of my conversational German. As she stepped off the elevator, she looked back and smiled, sardonically. We both knew I was failing her class.

I struggled in most of my classes, even Biology, a subject which I enjoyed. I had a good science background, knew a fair amount about living things, and thought I would do well in Biology, but I was not prepared to work hard in a lecture and a lab. And my World History class was not much better. My Professor, Dr. Nicholson, was renowned for his lectures on World War II, during which he would intersperse Adolph Hitler's speeches, in German, sometimes attracting standing-room only audiences in the lecture hall, including many former students. Dr. Nicholson's lectures often ended with a standing ovation. He would take an exaggerated bow, the Phi Betta Kappa key dangling around his neck, nearly touching the floor when he bowed.

Ironically, the one class where I did well was Rhetoric 101, a class with a reputation among the Black students at the Pier as a "flunk out" course. I had always enjoyed writing, even in high school, so I enjoyed Rhetoric. Yet my success in Rhetoric did not spillover into any of my other classes. The further I fell behind in my classes, the more I lost interest. Eventually, I began skipping classes to play Bid Whist with a group of Black students in the Student Lounge. Gilbert and Adams played Bid Whist too, but they were disciplined enough to make themselves push back from the card table, even if they had been dealt a good hand. I had a hard time leaving a good hand, and I flunked out of school after one semester.

When my father learned that I had flunked out, he told me that he was through paying tuition. From now on, I'd have to pay my own tuition. I was seventeen.

—18—

"Am I Fooling Myself Again"
The Teenagers

In the interest of full disclosure, another factor contributing to my poor performance in college was letting myself get involved with a good-looking high school senior named Sheila, who lived in Lake Meadows. It should be noted that I never dreamt of having any kind of a relationship with Sheila because I did not figure there would be anything about me that would interest her. Sheila was a "foxy" girl from New York City who still had her New York accent. She always seemed to have plenty of handsome, sharp-dressed, "Ivy League" style guys with cars (of all races) around her. In the past, I had been frustrated in my relationships with light-skinned Black girls, so I was prepared to live with the fact that I was not likely to be Sheila's type and made it a point not to fool myself into thinking that I could become her type.

On a Saturday night in September, I went to a party in another building in Lake Meadows. Sheila came into the party on the arm of her date, a clean-cut, light-skinned guy who did not live in Lake Meadows. A popular doo wop by a group called the Jive Five, *My True Story*, was playing on the record player, and I turned to my friend Butch and said, "You know, my all-time favorite doo wop group is still The Teenagers." Butch nodded affirmatively. The Teenagers were the legendary Black and Puerto Rican singing group that was led by a dynamic, fourteen-year-old singer with a big voice named Frankie Lymon. The group's 1956 mega-hit, *Why Do Fools Fall in Love?* earned the group an appearance on the *Ed Sullivan Television Show*. Sheila overheard me mention the Teenagers and abruptly tore away from her date's arm and rushed toward me with a wild look on her face, screeching, "Oh my God! I love the Teenagers too!"

For the next few minutes, Sheila and I stood in the middle of the dance floor, rattling off the names of Teenager's songs, while her date stood behind her, shifting his weight from side-to-side, trying to coax Sheila into dancing with him. Ignoring her date as we continued to talk, Sheila told me how impressed she was that I was familiar with so many of the Teenager's records, and that is when I told her that I had the Teenager's album at home. Sheila gasped, "Oh my God! You've got to let me hear that album... You can come over tomorrow and let me listen to that record." Looking dismayed, Sheila's date shook his head.

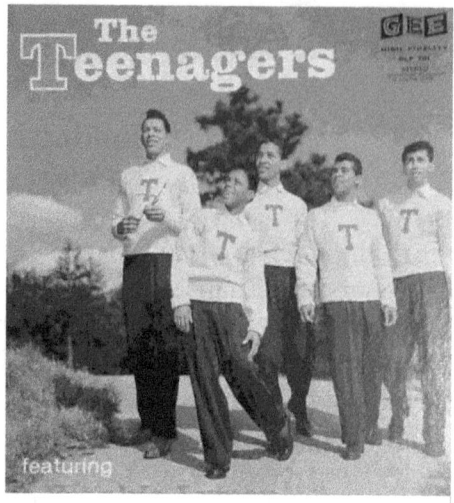

That's how it started.

Sheila's building was only a half-block away, so on Sunday I rushed to her building with my Teenager's album in my hand without a breaking a sweat, and for the next hour, Sheila and I sat on the couch in her living room, listening and singing every song on the album, as her mother walked back and forth past the living room, keeping an eye on us. Sheila pulled out some of her own 45s, and we listened to music for another hour before I headed home.

Sheila asked if she could keep my record one more night, and I said that she could. The next day, when I stopped by her apartment to pick up my record, Sheila and I ended up sitting and listening to the Teenagers' album all over again. She and I were enjoying each other's company, and I was developing a crush on her.

Over the next few weeks, I went to Sheila's several times after school to listen to music, and in the process, I "Putney Swoped" my way into a relationship. I figured that Sheila's suitors knew about me—Sheila probably told all her suitors that I was" just a friend" and they had nothing to worry about – and thought they could use my being around so much to "block" Sheila's other suitors. What they overlooked, of course, was that Sheila had so many suitors trying to "block" one another that I was getting to spend more time with her than the rest of them combined, and a relationship was bound to sprout.

Then one day Sheila asked me to take her to see the movie, *West Side Story*, for her birthday and I realized then that Sheila and

I were becoming "a couple." She became all I thought about. When I should have been studying for final exams over the Christmas break, I was thinking about Sheila. With the money I was making as a temporary letter carrier for the Post Office over the Christmas break, I just kept taking Sheila out and having fun instead of using some of the time over Christmas break to catch-up in some of my classes and study to get ready for final exams. When school resumed after Christmas break, I performed poorly on most of my finals and flunked out.

I never fooled myself into thinking that I had Sheila all locked up. I always knew that I would eventually lose her to some handsome, good-smelling guy who had a car. Still, it stung when I called one night, expecting Sheila to be at home, and her kid brother delighted in telling me that she was "out."

It was fun while it lasted.

—19—

> "Dancing is alright.
> But you can have a good time without dancing.
> Dancing won't make you cry. Crying is a strong emotion."
> *Dizzy Gillespie*

In addition to having to deal with the pain of my relationship with Sheila coming to an end, I was also down in the dumps about having pissed away my first semester of college. When I got official word that I had flunked out of the Pier, I just lay around the apartment, feeling sorry for myself until it was time to go work in the shop in the afternoon. Sometimes I would get out of the apartment and walk to the record shop on 35th Street to buy the latest R&B and Soul 45s. But after flunking out of school and losing whatever-it-was that Sheila and I had, the music was not doing much for my state of mind, with a long, cold winter ahead.

In March, Sheila's friend, June, who lived in Sheila's building, asked me if I would bring my collection of 45s to a party she was giving and DJ the party. Since I had not been socializing much, I decided that I would DJ June's party, hoping to reconnect with some friends. I picked out 50 of my latest 45s, including the best records for dancing.

Sheila came to the party, unescorted. We waved at each other, but before I could get to her, she was surrounded by her usual admirers. Most of the guys at the party were dressed in the preppy, "boss Ivy League" style that had become popular among fashion conscious young Black men in 1962. So when four "gousters"—high school boys who dressed like old-fashion 1940s and 50s era gangsters, with wide-legged, pleated pants, suspenders, large, Fedora hats, pointed-toed shoes and long overcoats—entered the party, they stood out like a sore thumb. (For reference: the bad guys who killed Cochise in the movie *Cooley High*, were gousters.) Given their belligerence, gousters seemed out-of-place at a college set. June explained that the reason they were at her party was because her parents told her that she would have to let her younger brother invite some of his friends to the party and, it turns out, his friends were "gousters."

Everybody at the party seemed to enjoy the music I was playing, including the gousters, who had their own unique style of "bopping." About half-way through the party, I put a stack of 45s on the spindle, pushed the automatic play button and stepped away from the record player to chat with some friends. I was talking with Sykes, when a disturbance broke out at the entrance to the apartment. From what I could tell, it looked like a group of people were coming into the party at the same that the "gousters" were leaving and incidental contact led to some predictable jostling and stares. I dismissed it as typical macho behavior by high school boys, and like many at the party, I was glad to see the gousters leaving.

As things settled back down, someone shouted, "Hey, ain't no music playing!" Since I was the DJ and responsible for the music, I rushed back to the record player, expecting to find that one of the 45s had gotten stuck and was keeping the next record from dropping. But when I got to the record player, what I saw took my breath away: all my records were gone! Immediately, I knew that the reason those "gousters" had been in such a hurry to leave the party was because they were hiding the records they had stolen under their long coats.

When I whispered to June that my records had been stolen, she got a horrified look on her face and threw her hands up in despair. Then she began scurrying around, trying to pull together enough of her own records to keep the party going, even asking Sheila to go to her apartment and bring some of her records to keep the party going.

I was so distraught that I told June I did not feel like being DJ anymore and was going home. With tears in her eyes, June said that she understood and gently patted my hand. Walking to my building, I thought about what I would do if I ran into the gousters on the street, but I never saw them. When I got home, I went to bed and curled up in a fetal position.

The day after the party, June and Sheila showed up at my apartment together. June surprised me by giving me $40 for my stolen records. At first, I was not going to accept the money because I did not want her to think that I was holding her responsible, but Sheila convinced me to take the money because it would make June feel better. So I accepted the money.

As soon as June and Sheila left my apartment, I headed to the record shop on 35th Street, intent on replacing as many of my stolen 45s as I could. While walking to the record shop, as I thought about all that had happened to me in the last month, from flunking out of school to losing my girlfriend and now, losing my record collection, I had a revelation: Instead of trying to replace records like *Ya Ya* or *The Roach*, I wanted to hear something more reflective, something like Miles Davis's *Some Day My Prince Will Come*, the tune that I heard that night at Norman's. When I got to 35th and South Park, I passed up the record shop and took a jitney cab to 59th Street and went to Met Records, a record store known for its inventory of jazz records. My transformation had begun.

As soon as I entered Met Records, I asked the proprietor, Maury Abrams, if he had *Some Day My Prince Will Come* in stock. As fate would have it, Maury said, "I don't have *Some Day My Prince Will Come* in stock, but," pointing to a bin full of Miles Davis albums, he said, "I'll bet you can find something in there that you'll like." I flipped thru the LPs in the Miles Davis bin, bypassing some of the Miles Davis LPs that Norman played, including, *Sketches of Spain* and *Kind of Blue*. Finally, I came upon a Miles Davis album called *Jazz Track* that had a black-and-white photo of actress Jeanne Moreau on the cover. The liner notes explained that the album was the soundtrack from a Louis Malle film, *Elevator to the Gallows*, about an illicit love affair. It sounded like a painful love story, so I thought *Jazz Track* might be good for the mood I was in.

Having featured listening booths was one of the best things about Met Records, as they allowed customers to preview records before buying them. I took *Jazz Track* into a booth, excitedly took the record out of its sleeve, placed it on the platter and put the tone arm down on the first track. The very first chord that pianist Bill Evans struck on a tune called *On Green Dolphin Street* was so pretty, as it perfectly captured the romantic sound I was seeking, and without listening to any more of the tune, I lifted the tone arm, put the record back into the jacket, left the listening booth and bought the record. And changed my life.

I played the side listing *On Green Dolphin Street* several times before I realized that I was listening to the B-side of the record and not the soundtrack to the movie. I was glad I had made that mistake. *Jazz Track* is the first jazz record I ever bought. It is also one of the records I would want if I were stranded on a desert island.

*****

Chicago's protracted winter months are conducive to self-reflection and getting one's battery recharged and that is exactly what I was able to do, listening to Miles Davis and his remarkable sextet, *sing* my blues away. I began collecting jazz records as enthusiastically as I had once collected R&B and Soul 45s. It did not take me long to spend the $40 I got from June.

The more I got into jazz, the more I understood what Norman meant when he talked about Black people needing to broaden their listening habits. To wit, whenever I was in a record store, I observed the comparatively small audience of Black men and women buying jazz records, especially in my age group. It surprised me that Black people were such a small part of the jazz record-buying market. For me, there was no doubt that music I was listening to was helping me heal inside.

—20—

"I'll Try Something New"
The Miracles

Early in the summer of 1962, I was back to my old self. I was energized and getting ready to return to The Pier in the fall. In addition to working more hours in the shop, my friend Billy Armstead and I started a car washing business for Lake Meadows' residents. Beginning in the morning, Billy and I would solicit residents as they came and went from the parking lots. We also washed walls. Armstead and I garnered a lot of business, working from sun-up to late afternoon, and we made a nice amount of money. Later, after washing cars, I would go to the shop and work until time to close the shop.

Word got around that Armstead and I were making a lot of money washing cars, so some of our Lake Meadows' buddies set up their own car washing businesses in some of the other parking lots in Lake Meadows. By that time, however, Armstead and I had gone on to other jobs. Armstead went to work in a cushy job in his wealthy stepfather's real estate office, and my cousin, Poppa, hooked me up with a summer job at Follett's College Book Company's warehouse, cleaning textbooks.

Because Follett's paid me a lot more per week than my father was paying me in the shop (including a lot of overtime), my hours at the shop dropped to only half-days on Saturdays but Dad did not complain because I was making "good money," as he put it. I turned eighteen in July, made a ton of money and got ready to go back to the Pier in September.

Toward the end of July, I got home from work at Follett's, and sitting in the living room was my Aunt Ann, Uncle Jack and my 19-year-old cousin, MacDonald. They had flown into Chicago to visit family and were staying at a downtown hotel. It had been five years since I had last seen Mac, and he looked more militant than when I last saw him in 1957. Mac was wearing his hair in "a natural," a trending "expression of Blackness that had not yet caught on in Chicago. Mac looked the way I expected Africans from Africa to look... which might explain why Africa, Africans and African Americans were such a big part of his conversation. A Junior at UCLA, Mac was very bright, well-read, and articulate. Black people in Chicago pronounced the word Negro, "nig-row." Mac was the first person I ever heard pronounce it "neeg-row."

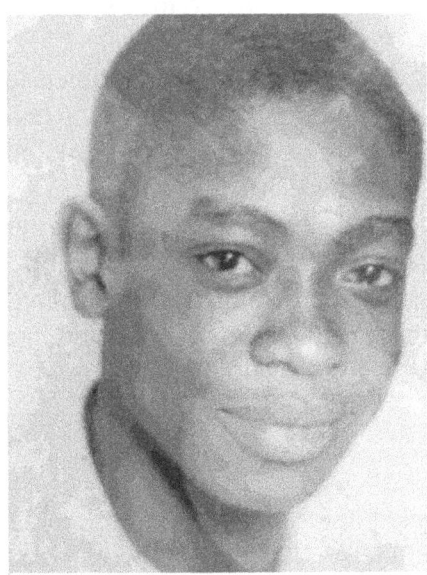

My cousin Mac in Los Angeles

As soon as I stepped into the apartment, Aunt Ann asked, "Well, George Allan, how is college going?" (My father's side of the family has always called me by my first and middle name because there are so many men named "George" in our family: besides me and my father being named George, Uncle Jack's real name was George Frazier, as was his oldest son, George Frazier, Jr. and his grandson, George Frazier, III.). I suspected that Aunt Ann already knew how college had gone for me because she and my father, her brother, talked often and he would have told her.

Unashamed, I spoke right up and admitted to Aunt Ann that I had flunked out of the Pier but quickly added that I was planning to return to the Pier in the fall. Aunt Ann began lecturing me about "the importance of getting a good, college education," and as she always did, threw in that her son, Frazier, had done so well in college that he was now a physician like his father, and how Mac would soon be a doctor, too. I noticed Mac smirking and shaking his head, "no."

The room was quiet for a few seconds, then Mac brightened and exhorted, "George Allan, you should come out to Los Angeles and go to UCLA with me!" Someone in the living room audibly gasped and cleared their throat. Quickly pivoting off Mac's comment, I forced a laugh, saying, "Mac, your offer is tempting but I doubt my grades are good enough for me to get into UCLA... and even if I could, I definitely could not afford to pay out-of-state-tuition in

California." I wanted everyone in the room to hear me sounding adult about my future.

Undaunted, Mac said, "George Allan, you could come out to Los Angeles and live with us, go to a community college like Los Angeles City College for a year, establish California State's residence, improve your grades and then transfer to UCLA." I smiled, thinking *what's not to like about that plan?*

A lot of my friends were going away to school, and I wanted to be able to say that I was going away to school too. If Aunt Ann and my parents were okay with it, I decided that I would take Mac up on his offer. Aunt Ann and Uncle Jack said that they had no problem with me coming to LA to live with them while I went to Los Angeles City College, and Dad said, "Well, that'd be alright, I guess." My mother's response was more cautious and measured when she said, "Well, if that's what you want to do…" her voice trailing off.

*****

For the rest of the summer, I piled up as many hours as I could at Follett's, as well as in the shop, and socked away money. In the meanwhile, as soon as Mac got back to Los Angeles, he shepherded my application, registration and enrollment papers through Los Angeles City College (LACC), and by the middle of August, I was all set to go to California. I bought a one-way ticket on the Santa Fe *El Capitan*, the same train I had taken to Los Angeles in 1957. A week before I headed to LA, I finally broke down and purchased Miles Davis's *Sketches of Spain* and heard the magnificent *Concierto de Aranjuez* playing in my head as the Western landscape rolled past.

Aunt Ann and Uncle Jack

—21—

"Do You Love Me"
The Contours

When the train pulled into the station in Los Angeles, Mac was there to meet me. His first words to me were, "George Allan, I've got a couple of places I want you to see before we go to the house." I rubbed my hands together and said, "I'm ready, let's go!" I expected Mac to take me sight-seeing to some of Los Angeles's famous landmarks, but I was completely wrong. Unlike Aunt Ann, who often said that places like South Central Los Angeles's mostly Black communities, Watts and Compton, reminded her of Chicago's, "dirty, all-Black, inner-city ghettos," Mac had a deep and abiding respect for all-Black communities and identified with The Hood, despite his bourgeois upbringing. During our ride around, an R&B tune called *Do You Love Me?* by a group called The Contours came on the radio. Mac pulled off the road, turned up the volume, got out of the car and started doing a funky version of the Twist, as traffic zipped past. When the tune was over, Mac got back in the car, pointed at the radio and said, "George Allan, that song should be the Black National Anthem!" I remember thinking to myself, "Wow, what a concept!"

Mac drove me to the UCLA campus in Westwood, where we ran into some of his friends. The first one I met was a scholarly-looking brother named Ron Everett, who Mac introduced as "a straight-A student from Maryland." Ron appeared to wince at the way Mac introduced him, and I sensed that Ron was not all that comfortable having his GPA be part of his moniker.

When Mac mentioned to Ron that I was from Chicago, Ron asked me assertively, "Brother, why do you suppose, with Chicago's long, history of Black politicians, Chicago is still so segregated?" I was impressed that Ron knew so much about Chicago. But I was embarrassed that I did not have a profound answer ready for him. Ron also had some interesting things to say about how White men still viewed Negroes as "three-fifths of a man." I did not know any "brothers" my age in Chicago who talked like Ron. Years later, by the way, Ron took a Swahili-Arabic name, Maulana Karenga, and created Kwanzaa, the annual celebration of African heritage in African American culture.

During that same visit to UCLA's campus, I met Mac's girlfriend, Rosalyn, a pretty girl with rich dark, smooth, rich-looking skin and a warm, radiant smile. When Mac told "Roz" that I was into jazz, she grinned, flashing her pretty white teeth, then spontaneously broke into John Hendrick's riff on John Coltrane's *Cousin Mary*. It was not lost on me that I did not know one Black woman in Chicago who could quote John Hendricks. When I asked Rosalyn how she got hip to Hendricks's *Cousin Mary*, she laughed and told me that "Cousin Mary" had once been on the juke box in the UCLA Student Union.

That made me recall that the juke box at the Pier was full of tunes like *Goodbye Cruel World* and *Runaround Sue*. I was in another world. Mac, Roz and I hung out on UCLA's campus for about an hour, with Mac introducing me to every Black person who passed by our table.

A "brother" named Willie stopped at the table and complained that he had just come from a class where he had seen a picture in which a Black man had been caricaturized as a monkey. Everybody at the table chimed in on the subject and then Willie said, "Just remember, if you shave a chimpanzee and put some dark glasses and clothes on him, you will have a creature with pink skin, straight hair and thin lips, in other words, a White man!" Everybody laughed. I was being exposed to a whole new way of looking at race.

Aunt Ann and Uncle Jack lived in a beautiful, ranch style home with a swimming pool on Southridge in View Park Hills, one of the wealthier, African American enclaves in Los Angeles. Aunt Ann's house was a pretty good distance from the LA City College campus, but I was used to riding public transportation long distances in Chicago, so I did not give the matter a second thought.

When I asked Mac about possible bus routes to City College, though, he told me that he had arranged for me to ride to school with a guy called "Sides" who lived down the street and was also attending City. Sides drove an Austin-Healey convertible. At first, I was excited about riding in a convertible for the first time in my life but, on the morning that George came by to pick me up, the top was down, even though the morning air was chilly. I did not complain.

When I got in the car, George shifted the car to the "Neutual" gear and let the car coast for nearly a mile, down a winding street through View Park Hills. When we got to the bottom of a hill, George popped the car into gear and accelerated into the speeding, morning rush hour traffic. It was scary, but again, I did not complain. The next time I rode with George, he pulled the exact, same stunt— coasted down the hill in Neutral then surged out into traffic.

When I asked George why he was driving that way, he explained that he was conserving gas. I offered to pay for his gas, but George smiled and said, "Oh, no, that won't be necessary…I'm going that way, anyway." I rode with George two more times before I lied and told him that my schedule had changed so I had to leave earlier for school and would be taking the bus to school. George just shrugged. "Okay," he said, "but if you ever need a ride, let me know." I was relieved to have escaped with my life.

—22—

"Surfin' USA"
The Beach Boys

The first time I stepped on to the LA City College campus, I had a new lease on life. The campus was bright and sunny and looked just like the photo on the recruiting brochure, featuring a diverse group of students, Black, White, Hispanic, Asians, Middle Easterners, Africans et al. I also saw my first, real-life surfers: shaggy-haired White boys with reddish-orange suntans, wearing T-shirts and shorts and low-quarter Converse gym shoes with no socks.

On a cool morning my second week at LACC, a White girl with short hair, high cheekbones and a pouty mouth named Shane came up to me in the Student Union and told me how much she liked the sweater I was wearing. She asked me where I had bought the sweater and, when I told her that I had bought my sweater in Chicago, where I was from, it led to a conversation. When I told her that I was living in LA with my aunt, uncle and cousin Mac, it turned out Shane had known Mac in high school.

Shane offered to help me find my way around LA and we exchanged phone numbers. I ended up calling Shane a couple times but that is as far as things went. I never told Mac that I knew Shane— not after the way I heard Mac and his friends criticize "brothers who mess around with White girls." Back in Chicago, I knew "brothers" who were always looking *for* White girls, but the group of "brothers" Mac introduced me to in LA were entirely different. One of Mac's friends, referred to White women as "beasts."

That same week, I was sitting in the Student Union when a White guy with dark rings under his eyes (which made him look sleepy) walked past me, carrying several jazz albums under his arm. I stopped him, told him I was from Chicago and asked him for a recommendation on where to shop for jazz. The guy's name was Romeo, and it turned out that, he had gone to LA High with Mac too. That night, when I asked Mac if he remembered Romeo, he said, "Yes... that guy who looks like a panda."

As jazz enthusiasts will do, Romeo and I stood and chatted about our favorite artists and recordings. When Miles Davis's name came up, I told Romeo how I did not like *Sketches of Spain* initially. Romeo said he had always liked the record, but he had been forced to stop playing it because it reminded his mother of the *old country* and made her cry. I never asked Romeo about the "old country."

Romeo had a car, and one day we agreed to leave campus together to go record shopping. As soon as my class ended, I walked across campus to meet Romeo, coming from his class. As I approached the building, I saw Romeo engaged in an animated conversation with a good-looking Black woman.

He introduced me to the sister, whose name was Florence LaRue. Romeo laughed and said, "Florence keeps telling me she's a jazz singer, but I keep telling her that she's really a pop singer." Florence put her hand on her hip in exaggerated fashion, and said, "Now, look..." and she and Romeo both dissolved into laughter. Finally, Florence waved her hand, turned her back to Romeo and strutted away, saying, "Boy, I can't talk to you!"

Romeo called out to her, "See you tomorrow. Now, go home and listen to some Ella Fitzgerald!" Florence looked back and laughed. I had never thought about the difference between a pop singer and a jazz singer, but upon reflection, there might have been a difference. Either way, Florence got the last laugh because she became a member of The Fifth Dimension, a fabulously successful "pop" group.

One day, Mac surprised me with tickets to see comedian Dick Gregory. Mac was taking Roz, so I asked a "sister" named Yvonne to be my date. She and I had been friendly as she was in my Anthropology class. We had excellent seats. A jazz group, The Curtis Amy Quartet, opened the show and performed for about forty-five minutes. When Amy's set ended, there was a brief intermission. When I asked Yvonne what she thought about Amy's set, she said she "didn't really like it. I don't like it when they play all those notes. I like music I can dance to." So much for finding a "sister" who was into the music!

Within our party, reviews of the Curtis Amy Quartet were mixed, but we all loved Dick Gregory's performance. I especially liked the way Gregory could talk about race in "polite, White company." At one point during his performance, Gregory shaded his eyes and looked up at the balcony, where most of the Black people were seated in the audience, then looked directly at our party and said "Whew! Y'all, I thought it was 'just us' in here…" My favorite Gregory line of the night was when he quipped, "You know, segregation is not all bad. In a head-on collision, the folks 'in the back of the bus' don't get hurt!"

—23—

"Freedom Sound"
The Jazz Crusaders

A short time after seeing Dick Gregory, I was exposed to another iconic Black figure, boxer Cassius Clay. After winning a Gold Medal at the 1960 Olympics, Clay—who had not yet converted to Islam and changed his name to Muhammad Ali—was in Los Angeles, training at Big Bear Resort for an upcoming match against Archie Moore. A few of Clay's high school buddies from Louisville were enrolled at LA City College and Clay would travel the approximately 100 miles from Big Bear to Los Angeles to hang out on LACC's campus with his homeboys. The handsome Clay was brash and charismatic, and whenever he showed up on City's campus, he attracted hordes of students of all races and nationalities, who followed the Olympic hero across campus as he talked, incessantly.

I joined the crowd following Clay across campus a couple times, and I always found him entertaining, but thought-provoking. As a rule, I tended to tamp down hero worship, but I did appreciate how there was meaning behind Clay's bravado, like when he referred to a beautiful, dark skin sister as "a Nubian princess." It was the first time I had ever heard the word Nubian.

Many older Black men from my father's generation were turned off by Clay's boastfulness—Clay liked to talk about how pretty he was and, along with singer and actor Harry Belafonte, Clay was one of the first Black men who White people recognized as handsome—but Dad liked Clay and predicted that, "one of these days, he could be as big a deal as Paul Robeson."

In late October of 1962, news reports blared that a US spy plane had confirmed the presence of Russian nuclear missiles off the coast of Cuba. United States President John F. Kennedy announced that the United States would not permit offensive weapons to be delivered to Cuba and demanded that the missiles be dismantled. Initially, the Soviet Union refused to remove the missiles, and it appeared that the US and the Soviet Union were on the brink of nuclear war.

It made me wonder if I would ever see my mother and father again, which was the scariest thought I ever had. The Cuban Missile Crisis was resolved, but I never forgot how it felt to come so close to the end of the world. Soon after that matter was resolved, I noticed a tall statuesque sister walking across City's campus. There was something familiar about the way the sister walked, and as she got closer, I remembered where I had seen that gait before.

It was Alice Jean, the girl at Harlan High School in Chicago who I would have asked to the Prom had she not "disappeared" at the start of my senior year. Now I knew where Alice had gone. Alice recognized me and we ran toward each other and embraced like long lost relatives. Alice explained how in the summer of 1960 her father had received and accepted a great job offer in LA, and she and her family had to pack up and leave Chicago in a hurry. Alice said she did not even have time to say goodbye to friends.

Alice told me that she had graduated from a high school in Los Angeles. "I can't believe that I have somebody from Chicago to hang out with," she laughed. Alice had a part-time job and a car and still lived at home and told me to expect to hear from her. My quality of life in LA had taken a dramatic turn for the better!

—24—

"(Nobody oughta be) Alone at Christmas"
Darlene Love

Without cold weather, there are no seasonal markers in LA like there are in Chicago. Consequently, I was not feeling the excitement leading up to Christmas that I usually felt. It just did not feel like Christmas was "on the way." Between the homesickness brought on by the Cuban Missile Crisis and the onset of December, I thought a lot about experiencing Christmas in Chicago. When I told Mac how I felt about going home for Christmas, he misunderstood me and sneered, "I don't understand why Black people continue to pay homage to a man who has despised them for 400 years!"

At first, I was angry that Mac assumed that my love of Christmastime had anything to do with a White Santa Claus or a White baby Jesus, because it didn't. I looked forward to Christmas in Chicago because of the snow and seeing Black neighborhoods lit up in Christmas lights, a traditional family dinner, and memories of being with my friends since childhood. No more. No less.

Without a doubt, my being around Mac had awakened me to a lot having to do with "race," but at the same time, I realized that Mac tended to turn everything into a statement about "race." After he talked about "the Whiteness of Christmas," I tried to explain to him what Christmas meant to me, but I don't think he understood.

Since Christmas break would only be for two weeks, I did not want to use four of those days travelling to and from Chicago on the train, so I decided to use what was left of my savings to purchase a round-trip plane ticket. Mac had flown many times, so he volunteered to book me a flight and I gave him the cash.

Buying that roundtrip ticket would not leave much cash in my pocket, but as soon as I made up my mind to go home for Christmas, I let Gilbert (who was still at The Pier) know that I was coming in and he went ahead and got my "temporary letter carrier" job back for me at the Post Office, so I knew I would be able to replenish my "pocket money," once I was back in Chicago.

For a lot of "brothers" and "sisters" in the early 1960s, California was the Promised Land, and I met Black people at LACC from all over the country, including from Texas, Louisiana, Louisville, Kentucky, Detroit, the West Indies, New York, Dayton, Ohio, and Hawaii. I even met "brothers" from Cheyenne, Wyoming. Still, I did not think it was possible that there could be anybody Black from Chicago on the campus who I did not know about. But a week before my flight to Chicago, I ran into a "brother" on City's campus who I knew from Chicago named Bobby.

He and I had not been close friends back in Chicago, but we "hung out" with a lot of the same people from that Lab School/Hyde Park "bourgeois Negro" crowd. Bobby's father was a prominent businessman and publisher of a well-known Black newspaper in Chicago. When Bobby and I saw each other, we exchanged pleasantries and talked about the odds that we would hook up at Los Angeles City College.

When Bobby mentioned that he was going to Chicago for Christmas, I told him that I was going to Chicago for Christmas too. As we continued talking, Bobby and I discovered that we were booked on the same United Airlines flight to Chicago on Friday, December 14th at 3pm. Excited Bobby told me that his father was going to be in LA on business during the week of December 1, and I was "welcome to ride with him and his father to the airport.

I had not given getting to the airport much thought, so I accepted Bobby's offer. He told me to meet him at noon on the steps of the Student Union. That evening, I told Aunt Ann about running into Bobby on campus, and she recognized his name, telling me that she knew Bobby's father. When I told her that I would be riding to the airport with Bobby and his father, she was glad because she had an appointment that day and would not be available to drive me to the airport while Mac would be at school and Uncle Jack would be busy at the hospital.

On the 14th, I was so excited about going to Chicago that I arrived at the Student Union before noon and waited for Bobby. But he never showed up. Both Alice Jean and Romeo had already gone from campus for the day, so there was no one around who I could catch a ride with to the airport. I realized I would have to get to the airport on my own. I had less than $10 for a taxi so, I set out for LAX on a public bus. Traveling slowly across LA's busy streets, I knew I was in danger of missing my flight.

While waiting on a corner to transfer to another bus, I saw Aunt Ann turn the corner, driving her big Cadillac. Frantically waving my arms and calling her name, she saw me and pulled over. I jumped in the car, explained to her how I had been stood up, and she rushed me to LAX, fussing at me all the way to the airport for "almost missing the flight…and losing money."

Thanks to her, I made the flight. As I boarded the plane, Bobby and his father were sitting in First Class. Bobby's father was reading with his head down, but Bobby saw me and gestured that he would talk with me later.

Once the plane was airborne, Bobby came back to my seat and apologized for standing me up. He told me that his father's schedule had changed but he had no way to contact me and tell me to meet him earlier. Bobby said that he tried to convince his father to go back to campus because I was there waiting for him, but his father would not do it. I would have felt better if Bobby had not told me that.

My first ever airplane flight was exhilarating — from the incredible take-off to the sublime, wheels down, as the City of Chicago, all lit-up for Christmas, appeared through a break in the winter clouds. The plane landed at O'Hare Airport, and as I exited the plane, Bobby waited for me at the bottom of the steps. He offered me a ride to Lake Meadows, but I told him my father was coming to pick me up. Bobby's father never looked up.

In 1962, there were not many Black people flying, and as I passed through the gate seeing no Black or Brown faces, I knew that there had been some sort of mix-up, because my father was never late for anything. That's when it dawned on me that he may have been at Midway, looking for me there.

Midway is on the Southwest Side, and in the early 50's, my father sometimes drove our family out to Midway so we could watch those big, prop planes, taking off and landing. But in 1955, commercial airliners started landing at O'Hare Airport, and when it added jetliners in 1959, O'Hare took over as "the World's busiest airport."

If my father was at the "wrong" airport, there was no way of knowing if or when he would figure it out or how long all of that might take. So after waiting at O'Hare for about thirty minutes, I decided that I would try to get to Lake Meadows on my own. With less than ten dollars in my pocket, my plan was to hail a taxi, tell the driver my situation and see if I could convince him that, once I reached Lake Meadows, I would be able to come up with the money I owed him either from my parents or from my neighbors. The very first taxi driver I approached turned out to be an affable Middle Eastern man who smiled at my situation and agreed to take me to Lake Meadows.

Forty-five minutes later, the cab arrived at Lake Meadows and the meter read sixteen dollars. I gave the driver the cash that I had in my pocket then to wait five minutes while I collected the rest of the money that I owed him. The driver laughed and said he would rather "go downtown and pick up a fare, and then come back in an hour to collect the rest of his money, so I gave him my apartment number and my watch to hold as collateral. We shook hands and he laughed again and drove off.

I let myself into the apartment with my key, and as I suspected, my parents were still out looking for me. I dropped my luggage and headed straight to Diane's apartment to start borrowing money. But before I could get out the door, my parents and my sister walked in. It turns out they had gone to Midway Airport and when I told my father how I had finagled the taxi ride home, he gave me the money to pay the balance of the fare. Thirty minutes later, the taxi driver rang the doorbell. I hurried downstairs, paid him and got my watch back.

Between getting stood up by Bobby and his father and having my family go to the wrong airport, "Christmas break" was off to a rocky start. But I was home for Christmas. Mac would not have understood how good that felt.

*****

The Monday after I got back to Chicago, I started working again at the Post Office as a temporary letter carrier at 7:30 in the morning, delivering mail in an all-White neighborhood in Ogden Park on the Southwest Side of Chicago. Delivering the mail was typically uneventful, although it was clear that some White people were not terribly friendly when they saw someone Black like me walk on to their front porch to put mail in their mailbox.

I finished my mail delivery route around 3 p.m., then caught a bus to the shop where I worked with Dad until 8 p.m. Being back at the shop and in my old neighborhood rekindled remembrances of the Christmases of my childhood, which is exactly the experience I was hoping to have when I made the decision to come home to Chicago for Christmas.

I got the chance to catch-up with my buddies, who were all home from college, including playing in our "annual Ice Bowl" touch-football game. There were parties almost every night, from Christmas to New Year's. Bobby was at one of the parties I went to over the Christmas Break, still apologizing for his father leaving me stranded on the LACC's campus. I told him not to worry about it and to have a Merry Christmas and a Happy New Year.

Those two weeks at Christmas Break went by fast, and when it was time to go back to LA, I was not ready to go. I realized all that home meant to me.

—25—

"Saturday Morning"
Ahmad Jamal

My second semester at LA City College was not as much fun or as interesting as my first semester had been. Academically, I was doing okay, but emotionally and socially, I was not into it. Mac was practically living with Roz, so I was not seeing much of him. And with both Romeo and Alice Jean working longer hours, I was not seeing much of them either. Occasionally, Alice and I managed to get together on weekends, but I had a lot of dead time on my hands.

Clint, my buddy from Detroit, said he thought having so much dead time was depressing me and suggested I should do something. Clint had "walked-on" to City's basketball team and was urging me to try to do something similar. Briefly, I considered trying to walk-on to City's baseball team, but I concluded that my chances of being able to compete with White boys from Southern California, who had been playing year-round baseball all their lives, were not good. One day, as I was watching some guys working out on the track, I remembered I had always been fast, so I decided to try out for LACC's track team.

Track and Field was as big a deal in Southern California as baseball. LACC's coaches kept an eye on all the former, California high school track stars enrolled at LACC, so I understood why those coaches did not expect much from me in the tryouts. However, when the coach had me run 220 yard-dash, I surprised everybody by outrunning some sprinters with big-name reputations, including a California State champion and a former Louisiana State sprint champion.

My performance in the 220 earned me a spot on the team. But after my initial excitement at having made the team, things turned sour when Coach told me that City's team "already had enough sprinters," so he wanted me to concentrate on training and developing as a middle-distance runner. I hated it. Coach entered me the 880 in two early track meets, but with very little conditioning and no experience in the 880, I was not competitive. I quit the team.

I was at home from school on a Friday afternoon when Aunt Ann and Uncle Jack were getting ready to drive to Las Vegas for the weekend. Aunt Ann said that she and Uncle Jack would not be back home until Sunday evening, but she had prepared meals in the fridge for Mac and me. Then, she handed me a written a list of chores that she wanted Mac and I to do while she and Uncle Jack were away in Vegas. Most of the chores on the list were routine stuff like "cut the grass," "bundle yard waste" and "sweep-up." The only non-routine chore on the list was "paint the pool chairs." I took the list and Aunt Ann and Uncle Jack drove off.

A short time later, Mac called home, and when I told him that his parents had just left for the weekend, he told me that he was spending the night at Rosalyn's and would see me Saturday morning. When I told Mac about the list of chores his mother had left for us, reading to him, he said "Aww, that's not too bad," he chuckled, "we can knock that off when I get home."

I told Mac that I would get started on the chores first thing Saturday morning and that I might have most of the chores done by the time he got home. Mac told me to wait for him before doing those pool chairs. He said that he would find a spray-painter in the garage that we could use to do the chairs. I said, "I'll see you Saturday morning."

I got up around 7:30 on Saturday morning, ate a bowl of cereal and started on the list of chores. By 10 a.m., I had finished every chore on the list, except for the pool chairs, which I figured Mac and I would get done as soon as he came home. At Noon, Mac called to say that he was still at Roz's. When I told Mac that I had finished every chore except for the pool chairs, he laughed and said that he might stay at Rosalyn's one more night. "But don't worry," he said, I will definitely be home early enough on Sunday to get the chairs painted—before my folks get back from Vegas." I agreed.

Sunday morning came and went— and no Mac. When Aunt Ann and Uncle Jack got back from Las Vegas around 4 p.m., Mac still had not come home. As soon as she entered the house, Aunt Ann began walking around, and I suspected that she was checking on the status of the list of chores. After a few minutes, she came into my bedroom and expressed how disappointed she was that the pool chairs were not done. I explained to Aunt Ann how Mac told me to wait for him before doing the pool chairs because he would find a "spray painter" in the garage that we could use, but he never came home.

Aunt Ann said, "George Allan, I don't believe Mac would say something like that, because there is no spray painter in the garage." From the other room I could hear Uncle Jack say, "Oh, pshaw, Ann, I don't know why you can't believe that MacDonald would say something like that… I believe it!" *Good ol Uncle Jack!*

Mac finally got home around 7 p.m. and went directly into his room and closed the door. Seconds later, I heard Aunt Ann rap lightly on Mac's door and when he grumpily said, "Who is it?" She entered his room and closed the door behind her.

My door was open, and I could hear Aunt Ann say, "Mac, George Allan said that you told him to wait for you to come home to paint the chairs because you would use a spray painter that's in the garage but…" Before, she could finish, Mac interrupted his mother and said, indignantly, "I did tell him that!"

Aunt Ann was silent. Then Mac told his mother he would paint the chairs himself. Aunt Ann chuckled weakly and said, "I'm gonna hold you to that." Then Mac added, "And by the way, Mother, there *is* a spray painter in the garage."

Leaving Mac's room, Aunt Ann walked past the open door of my room without saying anything. I was glad that Mac had owned up to the fact that he had told me to wait for him, but it angered me that my aunt did not apologize to me, after implying that I had lied to her. At that moment, I decided I was going home to Chicago when the semester was over and never coming back.

—26—

"How Can I Forget?"
Jimmy Holiday

As the semester was ending, I briefly reconsidered my plans not to return to LACC, because the manager of the bookstore on LACC's campus recognized me from Follett's College Book Company in Chicago and offered me a job working in the bookstore on campus. But I called my old job at Follett's, in Chicago, and told them when I would be available to work, and Follett's welcomed me back. Then I called my mother to tell her I would be coming home at the end of the semester.

That's when my mother told me that I would be coming to a new home: my parents had decided to move from Lake Meadows because of a rent increase. I remembered hearing them complaining about "a rent increase" while I was home over Christmas Break, with Dad saying that he would "rather own than rent and "write-off some expenses on his taxes."

At the time, I did not understand finance and thought my father was doing his usual complaining about needing more money, so I did not take him seriously. Apparently, he was serious. He and Mom found a little townhouse they liked at 92nd and Cottage Grove, with "a yard big enough to have a little garden." So, I would not be coming home to Lake Meadows.

When the semester ended at LACC, I headed back to Chicago, and my job at Follett's, and I did not hint to anyone that I was not planning to return to Aunt Ann in the Fall. Mac drove me to the train station, and as I boarded, he said, "See you later."

I just smiled. I had a lot to think about. I would miss Mac, Romeo, Clint, Alice and even Uncle Jack, but I knew that I would not be comfortable living with Aunt Ann. I had to be honest. Overall, living with Aunt Ann, Uncle Jack and Mac, had not been t bad, and they had been generous in their support and provided me with an environment in which I was able to get myself together in college.

I thought about whether I should have let the emotion of the moment pass when my aunt did not apologize to me. But I decided to stand by principle.

As soon as I got to the new house in Chicago, I called my friends in Lake Meadows, eager to talk with my buddies, Armstead and Gilbert, and let them know where I was. Armstead expressed regrets that I had moved from Lake Meadows, but he cautioned that it might be a good time to go. "Fudd, man, get on with your life. You're not leaving much behind, here in Lake Meadows. Your girl, Sheila, is pregnant and nobody hardly plays ball on the field, these days."

The news about Sheila did not surprise me; I always figured that it was just a matter of time before she got "caught" playing footsie with some good-smelling guy with a nice car. On the other hand, I could not visualize nobody playing ball on "the field." That, I needed to see for myself.

On a beautiful Saturday morning after I got back to Chicago, I took the Cottage Grove bus to Lake Meadows. The ride took about a half-hour, and when Lake Meadow's high rises came into view, I got excited. As the bus approached 33rd and South Park, I could see the field. There was a lone figure stretching and doing knee lifts, on the field. I could tell by the way he moved it was Norman. I would finally get my chance to thank him for turning me on to *Some Day My Prince Will Come*.

When I got off the bus and started walking toward Norman, he stopped exercising and came toward me, his hand extended. "So, how was California?" he asked, brimming with insincerity. He asked me had I played any ball, and I told him that I liked LA City College and had opted to "run track."

His eyes widened and he looked at me incredulously. "Track!?," he exclaimed, "Who the hell can you beat running?" Norman laughed, churlishly. It was like old times, with Norman being his usual, insufferably egotistical self. "You never know," I joked, "I might be a little bit faster than you think…"

Norman turned his back to me and started moving away from me, taking small steps by placing one foot in front of the other. I knew immediately that Norman called himself marking off a distance for him and me to race. Sure enough, when Norman was, maybe 60 or 70 yards away, he began walking back to me, smirking, "We goanna race!"

I wanted to say, "Man, I don't need this crap…" but I just smiled, took off my leather street shoes and prepared to race in my stocking feet. Of course, "Mister All Star" was wearing cleats.

Just as Norman and I were lining up to race, Mrs. Brown, Gilbert's mother, happened to walk by, coming from the grocery store. She waved at Norman and I, and Norman beckoned her over to "start" the race.

Giggling like a schoolgirl, she said, "Okay, you guys," and raising one arm. "Get on you mark…get set…Go!" she said, bringing her arm down dramatically while still giggling. With grass flying from his cleats, Norman dug away from the starting line first, his six-foot-three-inch body galloping like a horse. Once I started, I caught Norman, within 30 yards, passed him with ease and beat him to the finish line by at least five yards. Predictably, Norman complained that he had slipped at the start of the race. He hadn't. Mrs. Brown walked away, still laughing to herself. I was glad she was there to witness the race.

That day in 1963 was the last time I saw Norman. When I started writing my memoirs, I looked him up online and saw where he had become a writer, filmmaker and college professor in New York. If I ever see him again, I still plan to thank him for turning me on to *Some Day My Prince Will Come*.

—27—

"Come and Get These Memories"
Martha and The Vandellas

Having put Lake Meadows in my rearview mirror, I was ready get on with my new life in Chicago. I even got "promoted from Book Cleaner to Order Filler at Follett's. I also resumed working at Dad's shop in the evenings and on weekends. And, despite riding home with Dad from the shop all summer, he never asked me if I intended to return to Los Angeles City College. I got the feeling that he was glad I was home so that I could help in the shop.

My friend, Billy Adams, and a "brother" I knew from the Lab School, Rusty Elliott, invited me to join The Saints, a social club where they were members, and I jumped at the opportunity. The club that Chip and Nicky were in when we were eleven years old had petered out, and I knew several of The Saints.

They were "good brothers" who were all in college, liked sports, gave great parties and were always around attractive girls. The Saints could not have come into my life at a better time, helping me to jump start my social life after coming back to Chicago. My new neighborhood was in Harlan High School's district, so I reconnected with some of my old, high school friends who still lived in the area.

One day, as I went shopping at the ma and pa grocery store in my new neighborhood, a pretty cashier named Delores said, "Hi, I'll bet you are George. Your mother was in the store last week, and she told me that her son was coming home from college in California. You look new to the neighborhood, so I figured you must be Mrs. Smith's son. Welcome home."

I could not have dreamed of a better reception. Delores lived a block from my house, which meant I could walk to visit her. She was friendly and nice, and we ended up going out a few times. In fact, Delores was my date for the Saints' Summer Party. It was great being back home in Chicago.

In June, my sister, Janice, graduated from Hirsch High School and was planning to go to the Pier. Jan was bright and always a conscientious student, and I knew that she was focused and would have none of the problems I had in my first semester of college at the Pier.

I was proud of Jan and yet, during the entire time that I was in LA, I may have had one conversation with her. Now that she was all grown up and heading to college, I was interested in finding out "where her head was" about a lot of things.

Trying to find a subject that she and I could discuss, I asked my sister, "What are some of the hottest jams that Herb Kent 'The Kool Gent' [legendary Black Chicago disc jockey] is playing on the radio, these days?"

Jan rolled her eyes and deadpanned, "I have no idea what Herb Kent is playing. I'm into the Beatles!" At first, I wanted to criticize Janice for putting a White band ahead of Black bands, the way our father had once scolded me for having a White baseball hero. But, since I had never heard the Beatles' music, I could not say much. By the way, when I finally heard the Beatles, I felt they were overrated.

It was not until the summer was winding down and fall was fast approaching that I finally told my parents that I had no intention of returning to Los Angeles. I told them that I thought I would be more comfortable back in Chicago and either planned to go back to the Pier or some other, affordable college in Chicago. Neither of my parents said much. It would have been nice to go back to the Pier with Adams and Gilbert, but even though my study habits were better than when I first entered college, I was still not confident that my study habits had improved enough to handle the Pier.

So, after after giving my situation careful thought, I decided to enroll at Loop Junior College (now Harold Washington College) in downtown Chicago. I picked Loop for two reasons: it was one of the newer community college campuses in Chicago; and it was only minutes away, by "L," from my job at Follett's.

—28—

"Found True Love"
Billy Butler

Despite how far I had come in terms of my perspective on "race"— much of it resulting from the time I spent in LA around Mac and his friends— I felt unfulfilled. College-aged Black kids all over America were standing up against racial injustice and trying to make a difference by going on Freedom Rides, sitting-in and demonstrating for change on campuses and in the streets.

I wanted to be a part of that. Admittedly, when I first went to college in 1961, I was not thinking about activism. My time in LA changed all that. So when I started at Loop College in the fall of 1963, my social-political antenna was up, scanning for opportunities to be active in the struggle for civil rights and justice for Black people.

Shortly after the fall semester began, I met a brother in the Student Lounge at Loop named Eddie Potts. I listened in as Eddie was telling a group of Black students about his experience at the March on Washington for Jobs and Freedom, where he witnessed Dr. Martin Luther King's now famous *I Have a Dream* speech.

Eddie spoke on how Dr. King's inspirational words should motivate all Black people to "get out and do something about racial injustice." Later, when I told Eddie that I had been thinking about how I could become more active in the movement, his eyes lit up and he said, "Then you should come with me to an NAACP Youth Council meeting."

Eddie probably noticed me wince at the mention of the NAACP. The venerable, NAACP (National Association for the Advancement of Colored People) organization was not as highly regarded in the struggle for justice for Black people by my generation as it had once been.

Established in 1909, the NAACP helped make significant gains for Blacks in the courts for years, like in Black people's fight against segregated schools. In the 1960s, Black leaders like Malcolm X and Martin Luther King and organizations like SNCC and CORE were not content in "hitting and missing" in the courts in the fighting for justice. The newer version of Black leadership was taking grievances to the streets. Eddie said, "Don't worry, the Youth Council is in the streets."

The timing was perfect. A week later, I accompanied Eddie to an NAACP Youth Council meeting in the basement of a church on the Southside, where about fifteen Black college-age members were busy making picket signs for a planned demonstration outside the Chicago Board of Education's downtown office.

The NAACP Youth Council was preparing to join other groups, (some Black and some integrated) to protest the school Board's use of "Willis Wagons," which were Public School Superintendent Benjamin C. Willis's answer to overcrowding in all-Black public schools.

Rather than allowing Black kids to integrate all-White schools that had plenty of classroom space, Willis insisted on mounting mobile classrooms in playgrounds and vacant lots to alleviate the overcrowding in the all-Black schools. He justified his policy by suggesting that utilizing "wagons" was better for "preserving the integrity of neighborhoods."

On the morning of the demonstration, I had butterflies just knowing that I was finally "taking it to the streets." I took a bus downtown to meet Eddie and the other Youth Council members. We had to wait a few minutes while we waited for a "sister" to show up with the picket signs in the trunk of her car. I was itching to join the fray.

Minutes later, a sister named Violet arrived with the Youth Council's picket signs. We rushed over to Violet's car and grabbed signs, joining the picket line that was made up of other groups. The sign I grabbed read "Willis Wagon = Illegal Segregation." Not certain what to do next, I asked Eddie and he said, "Just watch me and do what I do!"

Black and White protesters in the picket line had begun to sing *We Shall Overcome*, a popular protest anthem of the day. I had to mouth the words because I only knew the first verse of the song. The picket line was visible to the automobile traffic on LaSalle Street, and it was funny to see the reactions of the passing motorists. Black motorists tended to honk their horns or display a clenched fist out of open window while shouting, "Right on!"

Most White motorists, on the other hand, would just glare at the demonstration. It made me wonder why there were not more White people who regarded "illegal segregation" as a problem.

After the picket line had circled a few times, Eddie, another "brother" and a White female demonstrator who was not with the Youth Council suddenly bolted from the picket line and ran into the traffic and sat down in the middle of the street.

It happened so fast I did not have time to react. I stood on the sidewalk, gawking at the cars slamming on their brakes to avoid running over Eddie and his sit-in companion. A police paddy wagon came screeching onto LaSalle, stopping traffic. Four policemen ran from the curbs where they had been trying to hold back the crowd a that had gathered, began dragging Eddie and the two other sit-in demonstrators towards the back of the paddy wagon, occasionally hitting them in the leg with their nightsticks.

Eddie and the other sit-in demonstrators tried to let their bodies go limp, but the policemen grabbed them by their arms and legs and tossed them into the back of the paddy wagon like a sack of potatoes. Then the paddy wagon sped off.

As more policemen moved closer to the picket line, the protesters began to disperse, peacefully vowing to return the next day. The Youth Council protesters put their signs back into the trunk of Violet's car and several of us, me included, rode back to the Southside with Violet. When I wondered if I was going to have to kick in some money to bail Eddie out of jail, Violet chuckled and said that the Youth Council had a fund for just such an occasion and the lawyer would take care of that.

As soon as I got home, I called Eddie's house and, to my surprise, he answered the phone. Laughing, he said, "Everything is fine. The cops didn't even bother to book us. They just checked to see if any of us had any outstanding warrants, and since none of us did, they let us go and told us to stay out of trouble. It was sorta fun. You should have sat-in, too." I was not about to get hit with a nightstick.

Are There Black Neighborhoods in Heaven?

Bernie Sanders participating in a 'Willis Wagon' protest while a college student in Chicago in 1963

My cousin Marie (the sister in the dark dress on the right) getting arrested at a Willis Wagon protest in 1963

—29—

"Miss Ann"
Eric Dolphy

Every President of the United States in my lifetime — from Franklin D. Roosevelt to Harry Truman to Dwight D. Eisenhower — were older White men.

So when 44-years old, WWII hero, John F. Kennedy, the handsome, Democratic Senator from Massachusetts with a fashion-icon wife became President in 1961, both White and Black young people of my generation identified with the promise of Kennedy's idealistic image. Kennedy's famous quote, "Ask not what your Country can do for you. Ask what you can do for your Country" inspired and guided millions of young people towards activism and responsible citizenship.

Kennedy was also America's first Catholic President, which added to his immense popularity in Chicago, a strong "Catholic town," from Mayor Richard J. Daley to the City's large population of Irish, Italian, Eastern European and Hispanics.

Among Chicago's Black leaders, however, Kennedy got mixed reviews, because they saw his professed commitment to civil rights as "iffy." At one point, Kennedy had proposed a Civil Rights Bill, but when it became evident that, in order to win re-election, he needed support from Southern Democrats called "Dixiecrats," he negotiated concessions to Dixiecrats, including some avowed segregationists. Thus many Black leaders reserved judgement on Kennedy, despite his "liberal agenda."

In a way, 1963 was a defining year for civil rights in America. In January, segregationist George Wallace was elected Governor of Alabama, declaring, "segregation now, segregation tomorrow, segregation forever." That was followed, in April, by the jailing of Reverend Martin Luther King, Jr. in Birmingham, Alabama.

Then a peaceful Black student march turned violent when Alabama policemen turned dogs loose on the students. That was followed in June by the murder of civil rights activist and Mississippi's NAACP Field Secretary, Medgar Evers. In August, the March on Washington took place. Then in September, four little Black girls ages eleven and fourteen were killed in the bombing of a Black church in Alabama by White segregationists. There was much to protest.

*****

On a cold day in November 1963, I was in Loop College's Student Lounge, listening to jazz records being played by a Black student named George Favors. George would play a record and discuss the music with whoever was listening. He had just finished playing a tune by saxophonist Eric Dolphy called "Miss Ann" to a tiny audience of two White girls, two "sisters" and me.

As George began trolling the two White girls about how Dolphy's frenetic-sounding music reminded him of "White girls trying to fast dance," the red-faced Dean of Students suddenly burst into the Lounge, pushing a large, color television on rollers and shouting, "President Kennedy's been shot! President Kennedy's been shot!"

Within minutes, CBS Anchor Walter Cronkite announced that Kennedy was dead. One of the Black girls screamed and the other one looked like she would faint. A White girl kept frantically wringing her hands and hyper-ventilating, "Oh, my God, Oh my God!"

Kennedy's assassination seemed to set off a whole new wave of Black and White young people protesting social injustices. Among the social causes being targeted by protesters was poverty, world hunger, peace, civil rights and the growing conflict in Vietnam. And while all of this was going on, the concept of Blackness and Black Pride was emerging in Black communities, supplanting the terms with which I had grown up, "Negroes" or "colored people." Black people had begun to show fierce pride in their natural physical characteristics, from skin color to their naturally kinky hair.

In the Spring of 1964, I bumped into a bright young "sister" I knew named Cheryl, who was home in Chicago for Spring Break, in a Hyde Park bookstore. I had heard that Cheryl's older sister was dating a well-known "Black Nationalist," and I figured I might be able to learn more about "Black Nationalist thinking" from talking with Cheryl, similarly to the way in which I had been "educated" by Mac and his friends when I first arrived in LA… so I asked her out on a date.

I apparently got the time of our date wrong, because when I arrived at Cheryl's house, she did not appear ready to go. She was fully dressed, but her hair had not been styled and was still damp around the edges, as though she had just come out of a shower.

I apologized to her for having shown up too early and encouraged Cheryl to take as much time as she needed to get ready. She looked annoyed, but she put on a coat, whipped a scarf around her neck and said, "C'mon, I'm ready, let's go!" and we headed out to the bus stop. Yeesh, I thought, I'm off to a bad start with Cheryl.

I was relieved that Cheryl and I did not have to wait too long for the bus in the cold air, but as soon as we boarded the bus, I was reminded that I had probably put her in an uncomfortable position by making her leave even before she had time to finish getting ready, judging from the way people on the bus kept stealing glances at Cheryl's hair. It was not until I heard a Black woman on the bus whisper to Cheryl, "Sister, I love your hair!" that I realized Cheryl was wearing her hair "in a natural."

While Cheryl was younger than me, her thinking about "race" was way ahead of me. We talked every day while she was in Chicago on Break. When Cheryl went back to college, I typed her a long letter, picking up where we left-off in our discourse. I felt that some of my ideas about "race" were profound, and I mentioned to Cheryl that I might try to publish them in a journal like *Black Collegian Magazine*.

Three weeks passed before I heard back from her and, when her response finally came in the mail, I could hardly wait to read it. Excited, I tore open the envelope and began reading. I immediately noticed that something about her letter was oddly familiar: she had sent my letter to her, back to me, edited, with corrections and comments written in the margins.

I knew then that Cheryl was "out of my league" and thinking that I could impress her was silly. Cheryl, by the way, went on to marry a great artist, a man more than 20 years her senior. Like I said, "out of my league."

—30—

"A Love Supreme"
John Coltrane

Winter 1965, I finally got up enough courage to go back to The Pier. Since I was still working part time at Follett's, I considered enrolling at the Pier as a part-time student but, with the War in Vietnam heating-up, resulting in more and more guys my age getting drafted into the Army, I could not take a chance on being a part-time student since you had to be a full-time students carrying at least 12 semester hours in order to qualify for a "2S-Student Deferment" and not getting drafted.

When I started back at The Pier in January 1965, I was curious if there remained any Black students who had been at the Pier when I first started college in 1961, but I did not see any. It looked to me like there were more Black students (including my sister, Jan) at The Pier in 1965, than there were in 1961. I looked around the Student Union and saw three or four tables of Black students playing Bid Whist, while back in 1961, there were, at most, two "Black tables."

I knew my chances of succeeding at The Pier would be better if I did not spend much time socializing in the Union, so, whenever I went into the Union, I made it a point to sit alone at a table, away from "the Black tables." Sometimes I would watch the activity at the "Black tables" from where I was sitting, guessing which Black freshmen would not make it back to The Pier for another semester. I felt like a tribal elder.

One day, as I was sitting alone in the Union, a "brother" named Richard asked if he could sit at the table with me. He seemed like a serious guy, so I gestured for him to pull up a chair and we immediately struck up a conversation. Richard, it turns out, was a Music Major in school and a budding jazz musician, who was already "gigging" around Chicago as an in-demand jazz pianist.

When I told him that I was into jazz, we talked about the music for the next half hour. As soon as I mentioned that, at one time, I had played trumpet he said, "Man, you should pick up your horn again!" I told him the story about how our fledgling "garage band" fell apart when someone discovered a box of old porn movies in the garage. Richard laughed and repeated, "You should try get back into your horn, man. If you want, I can help you get back into it."

At one time back in high school, I had become pretty good on the trumpet. I played *Cherry Pink and Apple Blossom White* during a recital, and the audience thought I was "lip synching" trumpeter Billy Estes, the lead trumpeter in Prez Prado's Band that made that song popular. Over the years, I had thought about getting back into playing my trumpet, but that aborted "garage band" experience soured me. Richard's sincerity was inspiring, however. I was curious to see how far I could progress on the trumpet, so I took Richard up on his offer.

Richard lived in Englewood on the Southside, and the first time that I went to house to practice with him, Kirk, his younger brother who was still in high school, was sitting at the piano in the basement playing Thelonious Monk's classic *Round Midnight*. I was shocked at how well Kirk could play.

Then Richard sat down on the piano bench next to Kirk and playfully nudged him aside, saying, "Move over rookie...," and finished the tune. Richard was astounding. When he got up from the piano, Richard pulled a tenor saxophone out of a case and beamed, "Now this is what I really want to do." And from then on, when Richard and I practiced music together, he played both piano and tenor. My interest in playing music was rekindled.

Often when I was at Richard's, other professional musicians would stop by to practice. They always encouraged me to play with them, which told me just how far I still had to go to be at their level. Once when Richard and I were practicing, a musician named Salter walked in carrying an LP in his hand.

Without saying a word, he walked over to the stereo and put the record on. For the next seven minutes, Salter, Richard and I stood listening to the record. When the first track ended, Salter took his record and left Richard's house. He never even said "goodbye." Richard and I stood there in shock. We had just heard *Acknowledgment* from John Coltrane's *A Love Supreme*. It was an incredible experience. The sound I saw was Black.

—31—

"Again"
Arthur Prysock

In a manner of speaking, I did eventually succumb to the lure of the Black tables at The Pier. Richard and I were sitting in the Union, one day, when a "sister" with cute dimples named Clara asked Richard and me if she could join us. Clara usually socialized at the "Black tables," so I was surprised when she chose to sit with Richard and me. Maybe all the seats at the Black tables were taken? Clara, Richard and I chatted for a few minutes, then Richard hurried off to class. Clara and I continued chatting for a little while before parting and going our separate ways to class.

Clara and I ended up on the same bus after school and continued our conversation. I was on my way to Follett's, so my stop came first, but before I said goodbye to Clara, I got her phone number. I called her when I got home from work, and we picked up where we left off in the conversation we were having on the bus.

There was something about Clara that excited me, and before our conversation ended, I asked her out, and she said "yes." That weekend, we went to see a movie and I found myself "falling" for Clara. Early in my courtship of Clara, I found out that she had an ex-boyfriend named Larry, who apparently was not ready to give her up and kept hanging around.

One afternoon, when Clara, Richard and I were leaving The Pier together, Larry showed up. Clara seemed surprised to see him and said, "Oh hi, Larry, what are you doing here?" She then introduced Larry to me and Richard, but he did not acknowledge either of us. Instead, Larry took Clara's arm and said, "I'm here to take you home." Clara walked away with Larry, briefly looking back and waving goodbye Richard and I. Richard knew that I liked Clara and he grumbled, "Man, you should have kicked that dude's ass."

Another time, when I was visiting Clara, Larry showed up on the front porch and rang the doorbell. Clara answered the door but would not invite Larry to come in. Larry looked in the living room and saw me sitting there and started lambasting Clara in a loud voice. It sounded as though the gist of what Larry was complaining about was that Clara was spending too much time with me. As Larry's voice grew louder, Clara's father came from the back of the house to see what was going on. Realizing that Clara's father was angry that Larry was "causing a scene," Larry leapt from the porch, jumped in his car and sped away down the narrow street. Clara apologized to me for the disturbance and then said, "Now, where were we?"

Clara and I continued dating and I got the impression that Larry was no longer in the picture. Then, out of nowhere, Clara told me that Larry had enlisted in the Army and asked her to spend his "last two weeks as a civilian" going out with him and only him, and Clara had agreed to grant his "last wish."

When Clara told me that she had agreed to spend those two weeks with Larry, my first thought was, "What kind of Black man is enlisting in the Army, these days? And, perhaps, equally important, "What kind of 'sister' would pick a 'brother' who thinks like that over me?" For the next two weeks, I did not call Clara and only waved when I saw her at school.

At the end of "the two weeks," Clara called and said that we could resume our relationship but, in all honesty, I could not get past the feeling that I could not trust her with my feelings. It pained me, but that was the end of Clara and me.

—32—

"Footprints"
Miles Davis Quintet

My disappointment over Clara, notwithstanding, I felt good about my second stint at The Pier. I was still resisting socializing and adhering to my new-found study regimen. In the meanwhile, I did allow myself to think about my recent experience with Clara and had to face-in to the fact that I needed access to a car, to be competitive on the dating scene.

That meant I needed to find a way to earn enough money to buy a car, while still being a full-time college student and avoiding the draft. I resigned from Follett's and went back to the Post Office, this time taking a full-time job. Then I enrolled at Roosevelt University, a private, four-year college, located downtown where I could be a full-time student going to school at night after work. My first car was a 1961 Volkswagen "bug."

A week after I got my car, I ran out of gas in the middle of the Dan Ryan Expressway, coming from school. Were it not for a kind White truck driver, I might have been killed. When my car coasted to a stop, an "18-wheeler," driven by a White man, pulled up behind my car with his hazard lights flashing.

He got out of his truck, risking being hit by the 60+ mile per hour traffic, whizzing by. He told me scoot over, got behind the wheel of my car and figured out that I was out of gas. Then he went back to his truck and brought back a gas can. The driver waited for me to run off the expressway to a nearby service station where I filled the can with gas.

After I put the gas in my car, it started right up and the truck driver told me to stay behind him and he would lead me safely back into traffic, which he did. I stayed behind him until I reached my exit at 95th Street and the driver stuck his arm out of his window and waved goodbye, proving to me, once and for all that skin color is not an issue with all White people.

Late in the fall of 1965, my mother introduced me to one of her church members, a Black woman named Mrs. Syler, who had been a graduate student at the University of Chicago's School of Social Service Administration at the time that my mother worked there as a Secretary to the Dean. In 1965, Mrs. Syler was Director of an Urban Progress Center (UPC) in Chicago's federally funded "War on Poverty" program and, after talking with me for several minutes, she asked if I would be interested in being a member of her Center's Community Advisory Committee.

There were nine UPC's throughout Chicago, and the one that Mrs. Syler ran was at 46th and South Park, close by the neighborhood where I had grown up on 41st Street. The Advisory Committee, she explained, was comprised of community leaders and businessmen and women volunteering to advise on matters such as "improving employment and educational opportunities" for poor people in the community.

After I attended three Advisory Committee meetings, Mrs. Syler pulled me aside and offered me a full-time, salaried position working at the UPC as a Work-Training Counselor for the Neighborhood Youth Corps (NYC) Program, a job training program for high school dropouts, ages 16-22. The City of Chicago had contracted with public works departments such as hospitals, airports, transportation and the Department of Streets and Sanitation, to provide minimum wage job opportunities for NYC enrollees, and my job was to "hire" and counsel those enrollees.

It was my first professional job. At night, I continued taking classes, full-time at Roosevelt.

—33—
"He'll Be Back"
The Players

Coming home from Roosevelt University one night, I stopped at Walgreen's to pick up a pint of Black Walnut ice cream to surprise my mother. Inside Walgreen's, I spotted a young lady named Joanne, who I recognized from The Pier. Joanne was a slender, exotic, caramel colored sister whose ethnicity was a mystery among Black students at The Pier.

Some Black students speculated that Joanne was Ethiopian, while others and some argued that she was mixed with East Indian. Adding to Joanne's mystique was the fact that she never sat at the "Black tables." Finally, a brother named Casey, who had gone to high school with Joanne, cleared up the mystery, announcing one day, "Y'all, Joanne is Black!"

Joanne was behind me in the checkout line at Walgreen's, so I waited for her and told her that I remembered seeing her at The Pier. Joanne laughed and said that she remembered seeing me at The Pier as well, and she mentioned seeing me sitting at a table by myself. That gave me the chance to tell her that I recalled that she did not sit at the" Black tables" either and we both laughed.

Joanne and I walked out of Walgreen's together, and when I realized that she was walking toward the bus stop, I offered to give her a lift home. Joanne declined my offer, saying, "That's not necessary. I don't have far to go, and the bus practically lets me off in front of my house."

I told Joanne that I would wait with her until her bus comes and she laughed and said, "Well, that's nice." A few minutes later, the bus was in sight. Before the bus arrived, I asked if I could call her sometime, and she said, "Oh, what the heck…Why not?" and gave me her telephone number.

I gave Joanne enough time to get home, and then I called her. She laughed and said, "Boy, you don't waste any time." We went on to have a great conversation, covering a variety of subjects, from "race" to movies to jazz. And we laughed a lot. I felt good about the vibe that Joanne and I seemed to have, so I asked her out on a date. She said "yes" and we went to see a the thriller, *Hush... Hush, Sweet Charlotte*, starring Betty Davis. We had a good time that evening and we went out a few more times, over the next few weeks.

Joanne and I were hitting it off well, but I tried not to let myself get too excited about what felt like a potentially, "budding relationship." However, I gave in to my excitement one night at a party when I stepped away from Joanne to get her a Coke and heard her telling a guy who was hitting on her, "Uh, not interested...besides, I've got a boyfriend." It felt good to finally be thought of as a boyfriend.

*****

Christmas season was always a good time for connecting with friends through Christmas cards, and one of the first things I did when I got home from school or work was to check to see if any Christmas cards were in the mail for me. Two weeks before Christmas in 1965, I saw two envelopes addressed to me. One was a Christmas card from my old friend, Alice Jean. The other envelope was letter-shaped and did not look like a Christmas card envelope. So, out of curiosity, I opened the letter-sized envelope, first, without checking the return address and started reading the letter which began, "Greetings..."

My first reaction was that the letter had to be a mistake or a joke. Since "the Viet Nam buildup," I had been careful to make certain that I was carrying the required number of semester hours in school to qualify for 2-S" student deferment" and avoid getting drafted. Which is why I figured that a letter informing me that I had been drafted and scheduled to be inducted into the Army in February 1966 had to be a mistake. Or a joke.

Right away I called Selective Service, the agency in charge of the military draft. I asked the woman I spoke with at Selective Service why I had been drafted, since I had a 2-S Student Deferment. The woman put me on hold for a few minutes then came back to the phone and said, dryly, "Mr. Smith, our records do not show that you have a 2-S Deferment."

Over the next several minutes, the woman at Selective Service and I went back and forth until she figured out that I had pre-registered for 6 semester hours at Roosevelt then added 6 more hours on the first day of the new semester, for a total of 12 semester hours. Apparently, Selective Service "saw" only the 6, pre-registered hours and not the 6 hours I added later.

The woman at the draft board said, "Sorry. There is nothing we can do." In desperation, I asked the woman if I was entitled to some sort of exemption because I worked helping poor people and she deadpanned, "You're kidding, right?"

When I got a draft notice, my life flashed before me. Would I end up in combat? Would I get killed or, worse, would I lose my glasses in the jungle? It was not until I snapped out of my initial shock that I started to deal with the reality that my induction date was, in fact, only weeks away.

I had several reasons for not wanting to get drafted. First, I was not all that patriotic. While I would rather live in America than in any other place in the world that I could think of, I was far from convinced that America's involvement in the Vietnam war was critical to America's or my future. Taking it a step further, the war just did not see like a Black man's fight.

Viet Nam had once been a French colony. With support from the Soviet Union, North Viet Nam broke away from France in a fierce civil war. South Viet Nam had been propped up and supported by the United States and its Western allies in their attempt to hold-off a Communist takeover of the entire country. My increasingly Afro centric/anti-colonial view of the world made me agree with those who questioned if Black men should even be involved in Viet Nam.

There was also the issue that Black men were being drafted into the military in numbers disproportionate to their numbers in the U.S. population, an indication of how far the tentacles of privilege can extend to systemically disadvantage Black Americans compared with White Americans. I knew quite a few brothers who had been drafted, but I did not know one White guy who had been drafted.

When I told my father that I had been drafted, he was still so angry about having been drafted into a segregated U.S. Navy during WWII, he immediately offered to help me "go to Canada to avoid the draft like some of the White boys have been doing."

I appreciated my father's offer, but I never seriously considered moving to Canada. Besides, the time to move to Canada would have been before I got drafted. Now that I was drafted, fleeing to Canada would have made me a fugitive in the United States.

Joanne and I had never discussed "the draft" or the war in Viet Nam, but since we saw so many social issues the same way, I just assumed that she would feel the same way as I did about the draft. But, when I told her that I had been drafted, she did not react much. I started ranting about the injustice of Black men getting drafted to fight against another people of color, on foreign soil, while being denied their rights at "home" in America but Joanne sat silently.

When I finished ranting, Joanne said, unemotionally, "What's the big deal... hey, you get drafted, we kiss and say goodbye at the train station, you go off to war, I write you letters, every day, while you're away, you come back, I meet you at the train station, we embrace and live happily ever after." I was speechless.

Giving each other small, inexpensive gifts over the "twelve days of Christmas" was Joanne's idea of "doing something different for Christmas" and, initially, it was fun. We were less than halfway through those twelve days when I got drafted, and Joanne seemed to delight in announcing that last six gifts I would get would be "little things that you can use in the Army," like a wallet-sized chess game. She just didn't get it.

—34—

"This Love"
The Joytones

Word that I had been drafted traveled fast among my friends. The Friday before New Year's, Joanne and I were at a party and people kept coming up to me saying, "Sorry to hear you got drafted..." But it was my buddy, Wimp, who said, "Hey man, I heard you got drafted. What are you going to do?" I told Wimp that Selective Service had told me that there was nothing that I could do.

Wimp said, "The National Guard Armory at 52nd and Cottage Grove just opened a new Battalion. I signed up! They've still got openings. You should see if you can get into the National Guard." When Joanne heard Wimp talking about the National Guard, she interjected, "What? You mean and be like one of those 'weekend warriors?' God, I hope not..." I wondered what Joanne was implying about me.

Wimp ignored Joanne's comment and went on to explain how enlisting in the National Guard would work. "When you get drafted, you have to go into the Army for two years," Wimp said, "but, when you enlist in the National Guard, you have a six-year obligation. First, you go away to spend six months in the Army at a base, somewhere in the country. Then, at the end of six months, you come back to your armory and attend drills every month for the next five-and-a-half years. Plus, every summer, you do to a two-week encampment on an Army base. I know that sounds like a lot," Wimp smiled, "but it beats having to go to and fight in Viet Nam. Of course, you could still have to go to Viet Nam if things go bad in the war," Wimp chuckled, "but let's hope it does not come to that."

During my conversation with Wimp, Joanne seemed rattled and increasingly impatient. When I told her that I was intrigued by what Wimp had said about the National Guard and I planned to check it out, she rolled her eyes.

Joanne's reaction notwithstanding, the day after New Year's, I went directly to the 52nd Street Armory to see about enlisting in the National Guard. The recruitment officer at the Armory confirmed what Wimp had said about there being openings in the Battalion.

"But," the officer warned, "since you have already been drafted and have a February 'induction date,' you cannot enlist in the National Guard, or any other branch of the Service, unless the Draft Board 'releases you from induction.' And you will have to go to the Selective Service office at 63rd and Western to try and get a release. Don't be surprised if you don't get one."

I thanked the officer and drove directly to the Selective Service office at 63rd and Western. When I arrived, it was filled with young men, trying to change their draft status. When I asked a uniformed soldier about getting a "release from induction" so that I could enlist in the National Guard, the soldier told me that first I would need to present the Army with a document from the National Guard, indicating that I would be enlisted in the Guard before the Army's induction date for me. The process was beginning to feel like a "catch-22."

I immediately headed back to the Armory to see if I could get that document the soldier at Selective Service had told me that I needed from the National Guard, showing the Army that I would enlist in the National Guard before my induction date. When I rushed into the Armory, the enlistment officer saw me and grinned. "I had a feeling you'd be back," he said. "I'll bet you need a 'letter of assurance' that you will be enlisted in the Guard, before your Army induction date, right?"

Then he smiled and pointed to a document on his desk that he had already prepared for me to sign. Pen in hand, I started to sign the document when the officer playfully snatched it away and said, "Well, first, you will have to promise me that you will come back to the Armory tonight."

"See," he said, "tonight's drill is the last time this month that there will be a doctor on duty in the Armory who can give you a physical exam. After tonight, February 17 is the next time that there will be a doctor in the Armory to give you a physical, and February 17 is after your Army induction date of February 10. That would be too late. So, either you come back tonight and pass your physical or 'you're in the Army, now…'" he half sang, off-key.

After I went back to the Selective Service office with the

promissory document, a soldier told me to take it into the Director's office to get a release from induction. The Director was a Black man with fair skin and reddish-colored hair, who I recognized as the father of one of my sister's friends.

When my turn came, I handed him the promissory document and stepped back. He did not bother to even read the document before raising his pen to sign it. While he was signing it, I leaned forward and quietly said that his daughter and my sister were friends, hoping that friendliness would take the edge off an otherwise tense situation.

The Director abruptly stopped signing my release and glared at me. At that moment, I realized that he may have felt that, by bringing up his daughter, I was putting him into a compromising position, and I wished that I could take my comment back, but I couldn't. My father once told me how "Negroes who hold government jobs sometimes act like 'Uncle Toms' by trying to show White people that they are patriotic and can be trusted not to do Black people any favors."

The Director paused for what seemed like an eternity before he resumed signing the release. Then, he contemptuously flipped the signed document in my direction, without making eye contact. I thanked the Director, spun around and left the Selective Service office, rushing back to the Armory with my release. When I handed the release to the officer at the Armory, he grinned and reminded me to come back that night to take my physical and get sworn into the National Guard, and that is exactly what I did.

Thinking that Joanne would be happy to learn that I would only be in the Army for six months, rather than two years, I drove directly to her house to tell her that I had enlisted in the National Guard. We sat in the living room while her thirteen-year-old sister, Julia, sat at a table in the living room, doing homework.

Joanne did not show any enthusiasm as I began to talk about my enlistment into Guard, but before she shared whatever it was that she was thinking, the doorbell rang. Joanne jumped up from the couch, went to the door and looked through the peephole. And, as she slowly opened the door, she sighed, "Oh boy, here we go…"

Joanne's 30-something older brother, Roy, pushed the door open and rushed into the house, knocking over the clothes tree and stumbling into the living room. He appeared inebriated and Roy's noisy entrance, alerted Joanne's father who exploded into the living room, shouting at his son to, "Get outta my house!!," Joanne's father exploded into the living room and began pushing Roy towards the door and the two large men grappled like Greco-Roman wrestlers. They crashed to the floor with a tremendous thud as Julia looked at me and covered her mouth in an embarrassed giggle.

Joanne's mother hurried into the living room and pulled, futilely, at the two men, yelling, "You two…stop it!!!" When the two men rolled under coffee table where I was sitting, I lifted my legs so they would not roll into me. Joanne looked at me and sighed, "This might be a good time for you to say goodnight."

I got up, stepped carefully around the two combatants, waved goodbye to Julia and left the house. On the way home, I worried about everyone's safety at Joanne's house, but I felt sad for her family. Joanne had never mentioned the tension between her brother and her father.

As soon as I got home, I called Joanne to make certain that she, her mother and her sister were okay— and to let her know that I cared. Joanne said that everyone was fine and hurried me off the phone by telling me that she would call me back later. She never did. That night was the last time I ever saw or spoke with Joanne.

—35—
"Since I Lost My Baby"
The Temptations

I attended my first National Guard drill a month after enlisting. It was January and cold outside when I started in the National Guard. Consequently, all of us new trainees began our Army training inside the Armory. We learned the language of the Army, protocols, how to take orders, line up, march and drill.

A month or so after we started training, we went to a rifle range to learn to shoot and handle M-1 rifles. Through all of it, trainees got yelled at and did a ton of push-ups. In June, we spent two weeks in training at Camp McCoy in Wisconsin. It was as though we were transported into "Army "world," each month, at the drills, then

My first National Guard "riot duty" on the West Side, 1966.

home, slept in our own beds and resumed our civilian lives, until the next month.

Most of the trainees in the Battalion were White, but there were a fair number of Black trainees too, including my buddy Wimp, the very person who first suggested that I enlist in the National Guard. Irrespective of race, most of the trainees who came into the Guard with me had done so for the same reasons as me: to minimize the uncertainty of war. Besides Wimp, I saw other trainees I knew, including Steve Harmon, who grew up down the street from me on Indiana Avenue, and a "brother" named Willie Nelson, who I first met in college in 1961 at The Pier, and a brother from Lake Meadows named Ron Vasser. Also from my old neighborhood on 41st was an "officer candidate" named Warren Allen. The Battalion Commander, Colonel Earl Strayhorn, was Black and a former Tuskegee Airman who also lived in Lake Meadows. My Company Commander, Captain Laddie, was also Black.

Many of the officers in the Battalion, Black and White, were Army veterans and had been in combat in the Vietnam war, the Korean war or WWII. They really liked military life. Several of the cadre, both Black and White, were policemen and fire fighters in their civilian jobs. The Army National Guard was not made-up of pacifists and weaklings, as the belittling term "weekend warrior" implies.

Captain Laddie did not do a lot of yelling at trainees, but he liked the trappings of "playing soldier," sticking out his chest, in exaggerated fashion, and pompously strutting around the armory with a swagger stick in his hand, or standing with a hand on each hip, like General George Patton, the famed, WWII General.

Captain Laddie was also prone to misspeak: one time, while addressing the Company, he crowed, "Men, if the shoe wears..." then, realizing that he had misspoken, he stopped talking to regroup but I heard Willie, who was standing in ranks behind me, mutter, "Yeah...fit that mutha fucka!"

When I enlisted in the National Guard, I was led to believe that I would be going away for six months at an Army base, such as Fort Jackson in South Carolina, or Fort Leonard Wood in Missouri. However, because so many Army bases were filled because of the "Viet Nam buildup," Command told us it was uncertain as to when we would be going to "six months." It was January of 1966 when I enlisted in the Guard and, six months later, in June, I still had not gone to "six months."

Attendance at scheduled drills was mandatory; an unexcused absence from a drill could result in discharge from the National Guard and immediate induction into the Regular Army, something that happened to a couple trainees in my battalion.

Are There Black Neighborhoods in Heaven?

My job as a "work training" supervisor for the Neighborhood Youth Corps program for high school dropouts.

—36—
"But It's Alright"
J.J. Jackson

"When I joined the National Guard, I anticipated that I would have to do "six months" active duty in the Army, attend drills in the Armory once per month for five years and go away to a two-week encampment every Summer. I also expected that would be activated to respond to emergencies or natural disasters or march in parades. But it never occurred to me that, as a National Guardsman, I would find myself on "race riot duty" in the streets of Chicago.

Now, I know you are wondering how, given the extensive media coverage of the many race riots taking place in cities across America in the mid-60s, in which there were images of the National Guard being deployed for riot duty, how I would not have expected the Guard unit I was in would not be involved in "riot duty."

Well, the answer is simple: all the Guardsmen I saw on tv were White men. For example, all the mages I saw of National Guardsmen on duty for the riots in Watts were from mostly White, Orange County, California. So in July 1966, when I got the call that my Guard unit was being activated for riot duty on the West Side of Chicago, I had to ask myself, *just what is it that a Black National Guardsman does, when the rioters are Black?*

There were two similar, but slightly different stories going around concerning what started Chicago's West Side riot during a heat wave in July 1966. In one story, a Black West Side resident went around opening fire hydrants in neighborhoods so that children could play in the nice, cool water which was a long-standing summer tradition in Chicago's Black, Hispanic and White neighborhoods.

The opened hydrants reduced water pressure in the neighborhoods and created a sloppy mess in the streets, so local merchants complained to the Water Department, which came out and shut off the hydrants. Black, residents, however, discovered that hydrants in some White neighborhoods had been allowed to stay open so the same Black man who initially opened the hydrants on the West Side, went back and re-opened them. The Chicago Police went after the man re-opening the hydrants and several Black West Side residents crowded together to protect the man from the Police, and rioting broke out.

In the other story about how the riot started, the Chicago police were chasing a robbery suspect through the streets on the West Side when the suspect tried to hide in a liquor store. The police followed the suspect into the liquor store and the suspect began yelling, "The police are trying to kill me! The police are trying to kill me!" A group of Black people surrounded the man to protect him from the police, causing the police to call for reinforcements.

Open hydrants led Chicago's West Side rioting in 1966.

Some people in the crowd tried to take advantage of the confusion and started looting the liquor store and other nearby stores. Gunshots were heard, sparking a rumor that a Black paramilitary organization was on its way to protect the people, so the National Guard was called out— my battalion.

Everyone in my Company was nervous as we were issued M-1 rifles and bayonets and packed onto 2½ ton trucks heading to West Side for riot duty. The all-Black West Side had a reputation for being even more violent than the all-Black Southside.

The biggest question on the minds of Black National Guardsmen was the extent to which Black Guardsmen would be expected to meet violence with violence, since most Black guys my age were somewhat sympathetic with poor, Black people for whom rioting was a way to bring attention to the ways they were being taken advantage of in a city as segregated as Chicago. For many Black people, looting White-owned businesses was "payback for years of price gouging and mistreating black folks," as one of the Black Guardsmen in my Company put it.

When White Guardsmen are involved in riot duty, they see their mission as "restoring law and order." But when Black Guardsmen are on riot duty they don't know whether to use the butt of their rifles to bust heads," as one Black Sergeant put it, or to "Just try to get the 'brothers' off the street and tell em to go home so nobody gets hurt.," as a different Black Sergeant put it.

When the National Guard trucks arrived on the West Side, I noticed people in the streets waving and applauding as though the National Guard was some kind of "liberating army." When a Black Guardsman named Dennis and I dismounted the truck together, a young Black man in the street pointed at us and shouted, "We glad y'all here…and even though y'all in that Army thang, y'all still Black!" I had not expected that kind of reception, but I welcomed it.

Dennis and I turned out to be the only two Black men in a squad of eight assigned to guard a lumber yard, a potential target for arsonists. It was a nerve-wracking assignment because the lumber yard was dimly lit and the all the streetlights around the lumber yard were out.

As the squad fanned out in the yard, a White soldier named John said that he thought he heard voices coming from a corner of the lumber yard, where there was a large tree. John and I walked towards the tree and, as we got close to the tree, we could hear voices coming from up in the tree.

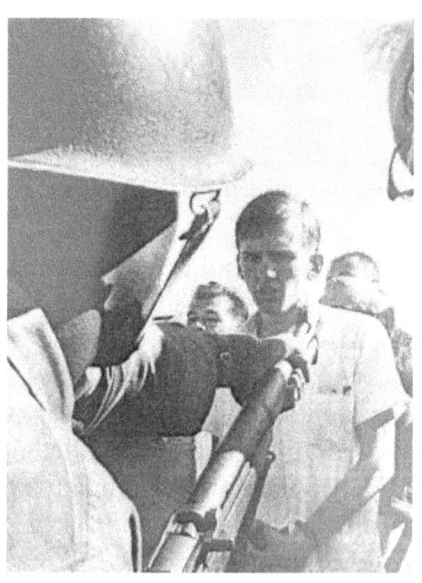

Riot duty in Cicero, 1966.

John pointed his unloaded rifle at the tree and shouted, "Whoever's up there better come down with your hands up or we'll shoot!" Then John winked at me. We heard more whispering, then a few leaves fluttered out of the tree, followed by three, small

Black boys who could not have been more than eleven.

The first little boy slid down the tree trunk, landed on his feet and raised his hands as though he was under arrest, his eyes as big as saucers. The second boy dropped to the ground, looked over and saw his buddy with hands in the air so he raised his hands, too, as he seemed to be fighting back tears. The third boy slid part of the way down the tree trunk, then dropped to the ground, rocking back on his butt and laughing. The laughing boy scrambled to his feet, started to raise his hands then lowered them, taking a step towards me and asking, "Hey, can I touch your gun?" John and I both smirked.

Trying to "sound like I mean business," I barked at the three little boys, "Go home before you get killed!" The boys lowered their hands, giggled and ran towards the rusted frame of an old truck that had no wheels in a corner of the lumber yard, as John and I kept our empty rifles trained on them. The boys pulled two bikes from under the truck, climbed on them with two boys on one bike, and rode out of the lumber yard into the dark.

My battalion was on riot duty for the entire week, patrolling the streets by day and sleeping in the bleachers in the Armory at night. My encounter with those three, "dangerous," eleven years-old boys in the lumber yard was the most action I saw that entire week.

On my last day of duty on the West Side, I was assigned to a squad that looked-in on a Reverend Jesse Jackson rally being held in an auditorium on the West Side. The only action at the rally turned out to be women swooning and shouting, "I love you, Jesse!" and "Marry me, Jesse!" while Jackson stood on the stage, basking in the adulation and slowly turning his head from side to side, as he looked out over his audience.

When I went back to work at the Center after the riot duty ended, a young man in my caseload (who knew I was in the National Guard) asked me if I had shot anybody while I was on duty. He seemed disappointed when I told him, "No!"

—37—

"2, 4, 6, 8, we don't want to integrate!"
"14, 12, 10, 8, you will, or you won't graduate!!!"
(Unknown)

When I was five years old, a building across the street from my house burned to the ground. After the fire was put out, all that was left was charred wood and rubble. I went to school with kids who lived in that building, and fortunately they all got out safely. But the ghostly images of that burned-out building left such an impression on me.

So in 1951, when I overheard my parents talking about how a mob of White people had burned down an apartment building in Cicero, Illinois, to prevent a Black family— Harvey Clark and his wife and children— from moving into the apartment. I was reminded of the horror of seeing that building in my neighborhood going up in flames, and I knew that Cicero must be a dangerous place for Black people.

In the spring of 1966, when a Black, 17-year-old kid named Jerome Huey was accosted and beaten to death by a group of White men in Cicero, where he had gone to apply for a job, I wondered if poor Huey, fifteen years after the Harvey Clark incident, was just too young to know anything about Cicero's resistance toward integration.

Unlike the mob of White people who burned out the Clarks and went scot-free, the White men who murdered Huey were caught and prosecuted but received relatively light sentences for "manslaughter." Many White and Black Chicagoans were so outraged at the light sentences Huey's murderers got that several protest demonstrations were proposed.

On Sunday, September 4, 1966, 250 members of CORE, the Congress of Racial Equality, an organization composed of Black and White members, decided to go into Cicero, "pray-in" at the spot where Huey was murdered and then conduct a non-violent march down Cicero Avenue.

Earlier in the summer of 1966, Dr. Martin Luther King led

marches into Chicago's all-White Southwest Side communities that were opposed to "open housing," as part of the Chicago Freedom Movement. White residents in communities like Gage, Marquette and Ogden Park were so hostile towards Dr. King and his followers that they stoned Dr. King, prompting King to say that it was worse than anything he had experienced in the South.

Those communities where King marched are all close to Cicero, so, when CORE was granted a permit to march, in Cicero on the Sunday before Labor Day, the Mayor of Cicero anticipated that thousands of angry White people, opposed to integration, would show up in Cicero to counter CORE's presence, so the mayor of Cicero requested that Illinois Governor Adlai Stevenson send in the National Guard to bolster law enforcement. Yes, one month after performing riot duty on the West Side, my National Guard unit was ordered to Cicero. This time, the rioters would be White.

CORE's "non-violent, protest demonstrations" were a bit different from Dr. King's: if a hostile White mob was to throw rocks at CORE's marchers, the CORE marchers just might pick up the rocks and throw them back. CORE's reputation for "not taking any crap off White people" made the "brothers" in my Guard unit contemplate the likelihood that hostility directed at CORE's demonstrators would bring about a physical, violent response from the National Guard, beyond anything we experienced on the West Side.

Seated next to me on the truck heading out of the Armory, on the way to Cicero, a White buddy named Jigelski said, "Smitty, I used to live in Cicero. Some of these people are crazy. But don't worry, I got your back!" I appreciated that. I think.

When the military vehicles transporting the National Guard battalion arrived in Cicero, the convoy mustered in the spacious, Western Electric Company's Hawthorne Plant's parking lot, from which we could see up and down Cicero Avenue.

Vocal, hostile Cicero residents were already massed in the streets. I'll never forget seeing a burly, Black Cook County Deputy Sheriff chase and catch a White male protester, pinning him up against a fence, and then pressing his baton against the protester's throat and lifting the protester off the ground until his feet dangled.

Cicero was already more violent than anything I had seen on the West Side. And the CORE marchers had not even shown up yet.

Unlike the West Side deployment, my Guard unit was issued ammunition for Cicero, and as we prepared to dismount the truck, a Black officer, Lieutenant Lawrence, ordered the battalion to "lock and load" and fix bayonets! And remember, "anything constitutes a weapon," Lieutenant Lawrence bellowed, "weapons, bricks, rocks, even spit...Shoot to kill!! Saddle up, let's go!!!" Awaiting my turn to jump off the truck, I worried that the crowd was so close to us that I might accidentally bayonet somebody.

Lieutenant Lawrence pointed to a corner near a light pole and told me to "Hold this corner!" then he hurried off to position other Guardsmen along Cicero Avenue. Our objective was to force the residents to remain on the curb and out of the street where CORE would be marching. The Guard was trying to form a phalanx to protect the CORE marchers from having physical contact with the hostile Cicero residents.

Holding my rifle at port arms with my bayonet prominently displayed, I stared straight ahead, facing the throng of people on the curb, occasionally telling them to "stay on the sidewalk and out of the street!" Colonel Strayhorn, the tough, no-nonsense Battalion Commander, fearlessly walked into the middle of Cicero Avenue with a bullhorn and a .45 automatic on his hip, directing protesters who kept trying to spill out into Cicero Avenue.

At one point, a White protester jumped into the street and tried to confront Colonel Strayhorn but a Black Guardsman next to Colonel Strayhorn stepped forward and bayonetted the man. Some of the Cicero residents helped the bleeding man stagger out of the street, but we never found out how badly the man was hurt. While I stood facing the mob, three White men stepped into the street and moved aggressively in my direction.

One of the men was close enough to able to read my name tag and he yelled, "Hey Smith, you're a Goddamn, nigger!" I did not flinch and told the men to "get out of the street and back on the sidewalk!" but they continued to come at me.

With my heart racing, I eased the safety off my rifle and made up my mind that I would shoot the first man to take another step in my direction. The men must have seen me remove the safety because they abruptly changed directions and rejoined the residents on the sidewalk.

The Cicero "riot" was over in less than an hour. CORE's

marchers went untouched, and when the march ended, they promptly boarded the bus they had rented to take them to Cicero and went back to the Southside. Once CORE was safely out of the area, my National Guard unit re-boarded our trucks and headed back to our Armory, leaving the Cicero police and Cook County Sheriff's Office to settle things down. It had been a wild, action-packed day.

On the ride back to the Armory, all the conversation was about the quick and decisive action that the Black Guardsman had taken, protecting Colonel Strayhorn. Someone claimed that they had seen a photographer taking a picture of the Black Guardsman in action and everybody on the truck said they would keep their eyes open for that photo. Many years later, I found that photo online.

Being able to act with impunity in the process of forcing those White people in Cicero to comply was an incredibly empowering experience for a Black man.

—38—

"Happenings"
Bobby Hutcherson

January is typically, one of the coldest months of the year in Chicago. The "Hawk," the ferocious, numbing, bone-chilling wind that takes your breath away in winter, seems to blow hardest in January. In addition, when the Hawk is blowing over Lake Michigan, it can create frighteningly severe weather conditions.

During Chicago's hot summers, the breeze coming off the lake can feel refreshing. But in January, the wind blowing off the lake can be warmer than the frigid Chicago air because the lake water has had all summer to warm up. And when the temperature off the lake is warmer than the cold winter air, it can bring lots of snow.

That is what happened in Chicago in January 1967. On Tuesday, January 24th, the temperature in Chicago was an unseasonably warm 65 degrees. Two days later, on Thursday, January 26, Chicago was hit with the most snow in its history, 23 inches.

Fortunately, Chicago does a great job of handling large amounts of snow, and by the following Monday, the city was back up and running as though nothing had happened. Recovery from a big snowfall has a way of making Chicagoans feel upbeat. It is as though just being able to see the sidewalk again after it has been covered with snow makes people happy.

That is how I felt when "the big snow of 1967" was finally gone. Unfortunately, my happiness was short lived because, in February 1967, I got my orders to report for six months in the Army. I was heading to Fort Dix, New Jersey.

While I was eager to do the six months and get it over with, I was a little apprehensive about what it was going to be like— for a National Guardsman to train alongside Regular Army enlistees and draftees.

I worried that, being a Black *National Guardsman*, Black draftees and "regular Army (RA) enlistees might assume that I had avoided the draft and joined the Guard by "knowing somebody" and hold a grudge against me, since only White boys were expected to benefit from "knowing somebody."

On the day that I was "ordered to report to Fort Dix, my father drove me to the train station in my car, telling me how he and my mother would use my car as a "second car" while I was away. I smiled at the irony, recalling the time when my father would not let me drive "his car."

There were eight other Guardsmen from my battalion heading to Fort Dix, including my Jewish friend, John, who helped me "capture" those "dangerous" 11-years old boys on the West Side. Besides me, there were three other Black Guardsmen from my battalion on their way to Fort Dix: Ronnie Vasser, a brother named Corky Penn and a recent Guard enlistee named Jimmy Williams.

When Jimmy introduced himself, he said he remembered seeing me catch the "L" at the Indiana Avenue Station, back in the mid-50s, while he was working at the fruit stand next to the "L" station. Jimmy said he had always wondered what I was carrying in a case when he saw me catching the "L," and I told him that I was on my way to my music lessons downtown and I was carrying a trumpet in the case." Jimmy grinned.

All the guys heading to Fort Dix that day had wives or girlfriends saying goodbye to them at the train station, except me. Watching Jimmy and his wife, Mildred saying goodbye made a lasting impression on me, and I remember thinking that one day I hoped to be in a relationship like the one they appeared to have. As the train pulled out of the station, Mildred stood on the platform, daubing her eyes, while Jimmy kept his eyes on her until the train curved around a bend. I felt for them.

—39—

"Get Ready"
The Temptations

My Platoon Sergeant Joe Fulton, in his "Smokey the Bear hat" during Basic Training at Fort Dix, New Jersey, 1967.

On the train ride to Fort Dix, Jimmy, Vasser, Corky and I stayed up all night talking. Everyone except for Jimmy had been in the Guard for a year, going through two "race riots" and a two-week Summer Camp, so we knew that we would likely have more "Army experience" than most of the men entering Basic Training or "Boot Camp."

In that one year in the Guard, we had experienced all sorts of "drill instructors" (DI's), so most of our conversation on the train that night was about how we needed to conduct ourselves as "trainees" to avoid the wrath of one of those "Smokey the Bear, hat-wearing," square-jawed, White drill instructors with a Southern drawl.

We also agreed that, as Black men, we would look out for each other, and not tolerate any racial "stuff." During the discussion, I said that I was as concerned about having to deal with older, Black, veteran-type, Drill Sergeants, as I was a Southern White DI.

I expressed concern that some older, Black, veteran sergeants at the Armory seemed to have contempt for Black men of our generation and are always going around saying stuff like, "You Negroes today ain't got what it takes!"

In the end though, we all agreed that we should not overreact to a Black Drill Sergeant either. And we agreed that our goal was to get through the next six months without problems and then get back home.

Normally, incoming trainees bound for "Boot Camp," first spend a few days in the Reception Center, picking up uniforms, gear and getting haircuts before being assigned to and reporting to our Basic Training, which lasts 8 weeks. In all, about 200 men entered the Reception Center at the same time, including Guardsmen, regular Army enlistees and draftees.

We learned that all of us would be Zulu (or "Z") Company during Basic Training. Since we were entering Basic Training during the "Vietnam buildup," all the Basic Training Barracks were full. So, we had to stay in the "temporary barracks" at the Reception Center, until we could move into our Basic Training barracks.

During those two weeks in the Reception Center, we performed details like pulling weeds and "KP duty," working in the Mess Hall. KP duty was an especially arduous duty at the Fort Dix Reception Center, because not only was Fort Dix an Overseas Detachment Base, but it was also located across the road from McGuire Air Force Base. That meant there were military personnel coming and going to and from the Reception Center's Mess Hall, literally all night long.

In our second week in the Reception Center, Jimmy, Vasser and I were on KP duty together. We bussed tables, washed dishes and cleaned pots and pans for hours. The sergeant in charge of the Mess Hall was a White man with a southern drawl who yelled at us incessantly.

After working without resting for several hours, Vasser told the Mess Sergeant that his "medical profile" required that he "relieve" himself every few hours. The Sergeant looked at Vasser with suspicion but growled, "You go to that John and do whatever you gotta do, then bring your ass back here!" Vasser dropped his dish rag and hurried off to the latrine.

Jimmy and I continued working, but ten minutes later, the Mess Sergeant looked at his watch and growled, "Hell, it don't take nobody that long to pee!" then told me and Jimmy, "You two boys go get your buddy and bring his ass back here!" Jimmy and I overlooked that the Sergeant had called us "boys" and rushed off to retrieve Vasser.

But as soon as we opened the door to the smelly latrine, Jimmy and I saw an open window, but no Vasser. Jimmy and I both laughed, knowing that Vasser had "gone AWOL" ("Away Without Leave") through that open window and, without saying anything, we scrambled out of that same open window and ran through the darkness to our barracks.

We ran into barracks and jumped int our bunks without bothering to get undressed and covered up with blankets. I looked over and saw that Vasser was already in his bunk, lying still and pretending to be asleep.

I kept expecting the Mess Sergeant to show up in the barracks looking for me, Jimmy and Vasser, but when he never came. I figured he just grabbed three other hapless trainees to finish our KP shift. Although I did not sleep much that night, I kept worrying that the Mess Sergeant might show up the next morning at reveille, but when a sergeant we hadn't seen before, an E-5, showed up in front of the formation at reveille and announced that our time in the Reception Center was over and we were off to start Basic Training, I finally relaxed.

The sergeant announced that we would get Army haircuts, then march to our Basic Training quarters where we would be assigned to our barracks, organized into platoons and be connected to our Platoon Sergeants. Basic Training was really starting.

The first stop, on the way to the Basic Training, was the Barber Shop, a large tent housing several barbers and barber's chairs. When the Sergeant announced that "every soldier is required to get his hair cut," Vasser freaked out. "They're finna mess with my 'natural,'" Vasser whined, while he patted his hair as though he was looking in a mirror. "My hair is my identity!" he said, defiantly.

Corky, who tended to take a conservative view on most subjects, deadpanned, "Ain't no Black Power in the Army!"

There was only one Black barber in the "barber's tent," and Vasser made it no secret he thought his best chance of preserving his Natural was to have that Black barber cut his hair.

As fate would have it, Vasser ended up in a line leading to a White barber so he, hastily, paid a White trainee in the Black barber's line $5 to switch lines with him. When it was Vasser's turn, he confidently bopped up to the Black barber, gesturing and telling the barber how he wanted his hair cut.

I heard the Black barber tell him, "I gotcha, bro!" Then, in a matter of seconds, the Black barber sheared off most of Vasser's hair. Realizing what was happening, all Vasser could do was futilely holler, "Hey..." but it was too late.

Angry, Vasser turned around to argue with the Black barber, who ignored Vasser and signaled for the next trainee in line to get in the chair. Vasser was crestfallen, but Jimmy, Corky and I just laughed.

Jimmy, Vasser and me in Army Basic Training at Fort Dix, New Jersey in July, 1967

—40—

"Mode for Joe"
Joe Henderson

Arriving at the Basic Training barracks, Zulu Company paraded like beauty contestants in front of four Drill Instructors in their Smokey the Bear campaign hats. The Company would be broken down into four platoons, with each platoon headed by one of those four DI's.

Two of the DI's looked like they were "straight out of central casting," with a White DI who looked like Clint Eastwood and a Black DI who looked like Denzel Washington. Two of the three had Combat Infantry Badges and two of them were paratroopers, "Airborne." These dudes were the real deal, and I tried to imagine what it was going to be like having one of them as a DI.

As each trainee's name was called, he was assigned to a platoon. Each platoon consisted of about fifty men. Once a platoon was formed, one of the DI's would stand in front of that platoon, "call it to attention" and "introduced" himself to the 50 wide-eyed trainees. Since my name was towards the end of the alphabet, I was in the 4th and last platoon to be formed, my worst fears coming into focus.

A wiry, unsmiling older Black DI, walking with a noticeable limp, moved towards my platoon. The old DI's dark skin was creased with a keloid scar that glistened in the sunlight and ran down the side of his face, past his cheek, ending up somewhere under his jaw.

His Smokey Bear hat was pulled so far down on his head that I could not see his eyes. And he constantly spit. The DI of the platoon I was in was the tough, no-nonsense, Sergeant Joe Fulton, who I heard about while at the Reception Center.

Fulton wore Combat Infantry ribbons from two wars, presumably Vietnam and the Korean War, although, he looked old enough to have fought in WWII. And he perfectly fit the profile of one of those old, super-patriotic Black veterans who could be especially hard on Black men who enlist in the National Guard. A veteran like Fulton could be a challenge for me, but for a "brother" like Vasser, who was hung-up on "saving his Natural," training under Fulton could be disastrous.

Fulton looked over the men of the 4th platoon who he had called to "attention," turning his head to spit, from time to time. I happened to be in the front row of the formation and Fulton leaned in close to my face and squinted as he read my name tag.

I looked straight ahead, holding my breath so as not to catch a whiff of whatever it was that Fulton had in his mouth that was making him spit so much. He startled me when he leaned back and, in a loud voice, roared, "Men, Smith, here, will be your Platoon Guide for the next eight weeks!" I made brief eye contact with Sgt. Fulton, then resumed looking straight ahead.

Being Platoon Guide was an honor as well as a big responsibility, because the Platoon Guide oversees the Platoon when the DI is not around. At first, I wondered if Fulton had chosen me to be Platoon Guide because he knew that, like all the Guardsman who had come to Fort Dix from Chicago, already had a year's worth of military experience.

But when Sergeant Fulton named Jimmy, Vasser, and a "brother" from Baltimore named Wilson who was "RA," Squad Leaders, it occurred to me that there just might be a little bit of "Black power" in the Army, after all: Fulton had put four of the six Black trainees in the Platoon into leadership positions. Once again, perhaps, it was time for me to recalibrate my thinking about "race."

All through boot camp, Fulton pushed the platoon hard, belying his age. He ran miles alongside the platoon every day. He climbed ropes with us and walked the parallel bars. He also did the same number of push-ups with one hand that we sometimes struggled to do using two hands. Sergeant Fulton yelled at everybody, including me, but the White guys were more intimidated by Fulton than the Black guys. Honestly, I found Fulton to be wittier than I did intimidating.

All four platoons that comprised Z Company trained together, and one day I got a taste of Sgt. Fulton's wit. During training, if you had to ask a question you had to state your rank and name and then ask your question. There was a "brother" in the Company named Davis who had an annoying habit of not only asking a lot of questions, but also adding a suffix at the end of his name, as in "Private John C. Davis, The Third," then prefacing his question with, "Sergeant, I hope you don't think this is a silly question but..." and going ahead and asking his question.

One day Davis raised his hand to ask a question, and when he said, Sergeant, I hope you don't think this is a silly question but..." Sergeant Fulton deadpanned, "Son, that's not a silly question...you're just a silly man!" The whole company let out a cheer and Sergeant Fulton had to quiet us by growling, "Knock it off!!"

Late one afternoon after training all day under a blistering sun, Sergeant Fulton had the Platoon kneel around him as he knelt on one knee. He removed his "Smokey Bear hat" and wiped his brow then he slowly said, "Men, I've got some bad news. While we've been out training, the First Sergeant informed me by radio, that you all failed today's 'barrack's inspection' because one of the windows in the latrine was closed, while all the other windows were open." (*Note: In the Army, every window must be open to the same height, or they must all be closed*).

Anticipating that we'd have to run extra miles in the hot sun because we failed the inspection, a collective groan arose from the platoon. Adding to everyone's frustration was the fact that the platoon had chosen a White trainee named Szczesny—who Sergeant Fulton called "Alphabets"— to be" last man out of the barracks."

The last man out would make one last look around, doing whatever was necessary in the barracks to make certain they were ready for inspection. As soon as we heard why we had failed the inspection, a couple of men in the platoon loudly criticized Szczesny for missing the closed window.

Seeing that men were expressing anger towards Szczesny, Sergeant Fulton said in a soothing voice, "Men, don't be too hard on 'Alphabets.' I can guess what probably happened. After you left the barracks this morning, some sorry son-of-a-bitch had to use the 'john', at the last minute, and he ran back in the barracks to take a shit. When he pulled his pants down, that cold air coming thru an open window probably hit him in his ass, so he got up from the stool and closed the window, then he forgot to re-open the window when he was done."

I smiled at the image Sergeant. Fulton painted of a shivering trainee, hopping over to close a window with his fatigues down around his knees.

Suddenly, Sergeant Fulton's demeanor changed. He stood up and slapped his hat on his head and in a defiant voice, bellowed, "Well men, *I* was that sorry son-of-a-bitch!"

The platoon gawked in stunned silence. Sergeant Fulton called us to attention and then he ran us another mile or so back to the barracks. I remember thinking, *Well-played, Sarge!*

—41—

"Groovin'"
The Rascals

Overall, I performed well the during the 8-weeks of Basic Training, and at the end-of-the cycle ceremony for the more than 1,000 trainees in my Basic Training Cycle (including draftees and Regular Army enlistees), I was named the "Runner-up Trainee of the Cycle," finishing second to a National Guardsman from Maryland who was a quarterback for the NFL's Baltimore Colts. Sergeant Fulton congratulated me, looking sharp in his Campaign Hat and gabardine dress uniform.

Jimmy, Corky, Vasser and I had the same MOS (Military Occupational Status) as Infantrymen. So, after graduating from Basic Training, our orders called for us to remain at Fort Dix and complete eight weeks of Advanced Individual Training (AIT) as Infantrymen, which was nice, since we would only have to move to different barracks.

I hated to say goodbye to a brother from Connecticut named Rodriguez, whom Jimmy, Vasser and I dubbed, "Papa Romeo." His MOS was Culinary Specialist, so he was heading to Cook School at an Army base in Virginia.

Papa Romeo had dark brown skin and wavy, shiny, black hair, and when we asked him about his ethnicity, he told us he was Portuguese. We joked with him that he was most likely Puerto Rican, but he was calling himself Portuguese because it sounded exotic. "Papa Romeo" was the Army's phonetic abbreviation for PR.

Although several guys from my Basic Training Company ended up in my Company in AIT, we also trained with a lot more Regular Army enlistees and draftees whose next orders would likely be in Vietnam. From the start, AIT was a completely different experience than Basic Training. For one, throughout AIT, I did not have any rank, like "Platoon Guide," so I was not entitled to any more privileges than anyone else in my platoon.

Another difference between Basic Training and AIT was that

Basic had been all about getting into good, physical shape and learning to think and do things the Army way; Infantry AIT was all about learning how to kill the enemy in combat.

My Company Commander in AIT, Captain Williams, was a youthful, not-yet-30-years old blond, sun-burned officer who had served in Vietnam, where he stepped on an explosive device that permanently left him walking with a noticeable spasm.

Captain Williams approached commanding troops as you would expect someone who was happy to be alive, constantly having fun at the trainees' expense, doing things like dropping tear gas grenades in the middle of unsuspecting, trainees (If you have never been tear-gassed, know that it not only makes you choke and your eyes water, but it also makes sweaty skin sting!) just to see how they would react.

One time, while we were training on a .50 caliber Machine Gun range, Captain Williams tossed a dead, six-foot King Snake into a trench full of trainees and laughed as the trainees ran out of the trench in terror, risking having their heads blown off.

Somehow, Corky managed to become Captain Williams's regular Jeep driver, which was a great gig. Being the CO's driver kept Corky out of the muck and mire of AIT's Infantry training. Vasser, though, was resentful of Corky's good fortune, complaining that "Corky never warns any of us when Captain Williams is about to pull one of his pranks. "Corky acts like an 'Uncle Tom'," Vasser griped.

Having been in a similar position when I was a Platoon Guide in Basic Training and occasionally privy to inside information, I understood Corky's situation and I told Vasser to be cool and not to worry about Corky, who I knew just wanted to get through six months and then go home to his wife. Vasser never lightened up on Corky, and it was sad seeing their relationship deteriorate, so close to the end of AIT.

During the eight weeks of AIT, I experienced only one incident that could be considered racial. During a pugil stick exercise, I was paired against a White soldier named Keith, who had been in my platoon in Basic Training. Pugil sticks are the long, padded sticks used in bayonet training. Keith was a thick, hulking tobacco farmer from North Carolina who referred to himself as a "redneck." Keith may have outweighed me by as much as 100 pounds, and as we squared off in our Pugil Sticks match, he charged, using his pugil stick like a club, trying to pound me into submission.

Fortunately, I managed to block his withering blows and avoided getting hit in the head. I knew that I was in the fight of my life against a White man seeking revenge against me because, as his Platoon Guide, I had been in charge of him during Basic Training. Keith exerted so much energy, bashing me with his pugil stick that he had to paused to catch his breath. With his stick slightly lowered, I thrust with my stick, barely touching Keith in the rib area.

Then the DI in charge of the exercise stepped between me and Keith and raised my hand, declaring me the winner. Keith and I were both stunned because neither of us realized that each time I blocked one of Keith's blows, I was earning points for a parry, and when I touched him, it gave me enough points to win. Keith yanked off his helmet and glared at me, his face flushed.

Jimmy whispered to me, "Man, you need to keep an eye on Keith, with all this live ammo around."

In retrospect, I could not tell if the fury that Keith displayed that day with the pugil sticks had anything to do with race. Maybe he just did not know what to do with a pugil stick.

During Basic Training, I remembered that the only trainees I saw Keith hanging with was a small group of "hillbillies" from North Carolina, and how, whenever I gave an order as the Platoon Guide, Keith would glare at me. I concluded that the ferocity he displayed in trying to coldcock me with his pugil stick was an extension of the anger he showed toward me in Basic Training.

I never got the feeling that any of the other men in Keith's group had a problem taking orders from Black men. On the other hand, Keith could be strange. A couple weeks after the pugil sticks incident, Keith broke into the Mess Hall overnight and stole a bag of left-over pork chops and some bread, providing a late-night-snack for everybody in the barracks. He even handed me a sandwich.

—42—

"Funky Broadway"
Wilson Pickett

    Without a doubt, the best part of AIT were the "overnight passes" we received almost every Saturday afternoon at the end of the week's training. With an overnight pass, a trainee could leave Fort Dix on a Saturday afternoon and was not required to be back on the base until reveille, the following Monday. Trainees who were from the New Jersey area sometimes had their family or friends pick them up at Fort Dix so that they could spend the weekend at home.
    Chicago, of course, was too far and too expensive for me, Jimmy and Vasser to go home on the weekend, so we took our passes, caught a bus at Fort Dix and took it to Port Authority in New York City, a trip of less than an hour.
    On our first trip to New York, the three of us did a little sightseeing. We stayed at a motel overnight and resumed sightseeing on Sunday, before returning to Fort Dix on Sunday night. On a subsequent visit to New York, we split up, with Vasser going to a disco while Jimmy and I went to a basketball tournament in Madison Square Garden. Another time, Jimmy and Vasser went somewhere, while I went to hear live jazz at the Village Vanguard.
    Whenever we used our overnight passes to go to New York, Jimmy and I would wear our shined, low quarter shoes, dress khaki's and "garrison caps." Vasser, though, wore his service cap and dress greens that he adorned with so many trinkets and badges he had bought at the Post Exchange that he looked like a General, walking down the streets of New York. Thinking that Vasser was a real Officer, the military servicemen we encountered would salute Vasser and he would "smartly, return the salute" and mutter, "Carry on!" It was funny.
    One Sunday, Jimmy, Vasser and I went to a New York Yankee's baseball game at Yankee Stadium. As the National Anthem was being played, everyone in the Stadium stood, except

for four, White, college-aged kids who were seated directly in front of us. Being servicemen in uniform, we were required to stand and salute.

One of the White girls who refused to stand for the Anthem turned around and saw us saluting and turned back to her friends and laughed, "Oh my God, they're saluting!" Jimmy and I thought the girl's reaction was funny, but Vasser was visibly upset at her comment. When the Anthem ended, Vasser vowed he would never wear his uniform again, while on leave.

While I was in AIT, I developed a friendship with an 18-year-old White kid named Russell. Russell was from Perth Amboy, New Jersey, and told me that he had enlisted in the regular Army, the day after he graduated high school. Russell wanted to become "a Green Beret," a Special Forces Commando.

At the beginning of AIT, Russell was gung-ho about the Army, but as the weeks dragged on, I sensed he was losing his enthusiasm. The change in Russell's attitude toward the Army noticeably changed the closer we came to the end of AIT.

Russell's state of mind could not have been helped by the fact that Jimmy, Vasser and I talked all the time about the things we planned to do back home, in Chicago, when AIT was over. One day, Russell told me that, if he had it to do all over again, he would not have enlisted in the Army after high school.

"I might even have tried college," he lamented. Hearing Russell having second thoughts about having joined the Army out of high school, I wondered how I would have counseled him had he been one of the NYC enrollees in my caseload.

At the end of AIT, Russell learned that his acceptance into Special Forces was being delayed and he was ordered to a duty station as an infantryman. A few months after I was out of AIT and back in Chicago, I got a letter from Russell, sharing that he was "in the DMZ, between North and South Viet Nam, and hearing gunfire." I never heard from Russell again. I did not see Russell's name on the "Wall" in Washington, DC, so I'm hopeful that he made it back home safely.

—43—

"Respect"
Aretha Franklin

When I got my orders to report to Fort Dix for six months, I applied for and received a Military Leave from CCUO, my employer. A Military Leave assured me of re-employment in the job I left or a comparable job, but when got out of AIT and returned to Chicago, I discovered that the job I was in at the time I took the Military Leave was still open at the Center. Wasting no time, I went to the HR Department at the agency headquarters and applied to reclaim my job with the Neighborhood Youth Corps. HR reinstated me and told me to report to the Center.

When I got to the Center, I learned that Mrs. Syler, the person who first hired me, was no longer Director at the Center. During the six months that I had been away, Mrs. Syler had been promoted to a big job, downtown, at the agency's headquarters, and the director who replaced her as Center Director was a Black man named Kenneth.

Kenneth's Administrative Assistant told me she could find no record of my having been on a Military Leave nor, for that matter, any record of my ever having worked at the Center. Fortunately, I had with me my old Identification card as well as a copy of my Military Leave papers. The Assistant then said that she would have to call me.

Before I left the Center, Kenneth walked in. He was a thick, burly ex-policeman and former boxing promoter. I remember thinking that he had an unusual background for someone in charge of a federally funded social services agency. I introduced myself and let Kenneth know that I was returning from Military Leave and ready to go to work. Kenneth looked at me skeptically and said, "Yeah, uh huh…yeah, well, we'll see." That is when I knew that I had a problem.

A week went by with no call back, so I called HR, and the HR Manager hinted that the Center Director "might not have been expecting you and may have to 'move some things around' to accommodate your return." My conversation with HR sounded political to me, like the HR Manager was trying to hide the fact that my return from Military Leave may have "put a wrench" into Kenneth's plans to somehow leverage my job for his political advantage, like turning my position into a "patronage job," a staple of Chicago politics.

It was another two weeks before I was called in to my NYC job at the Center. Kenneth was never welcoming toward me. In fact, at times, he showed outright contempt for the work we were doing in the NYC program.

Once, he called a "mandatory, all-staff, emergency meeting" at the Center, just as I was sitting down with a 16-year-old-girl who needed a job to be able to pay for child-care, allowing her to finish high school, after having a baby. I sent word to Kenneth that I would be five minutes late to the meeting so that I could finish helping the girl.

In fact, I finished counseling the girl and arrived at the meeting less than five minutes late, but when I walked into the meeting, there was nothing going on. When Kenneth saw me walk in, he said, "guess we can get started now. George has finally blessed us with his presence," with a scowl on his face.

One day I thought I had a chance to improve my relationship with Kenneth. There was a lot of commotion in the Center, so I went outside my second-floor office to see Kenneth escorting Heavyweight Boxing Champion Muhammad Ali through a huge crowd that had gathered in the Center.

As Ali and Kenneth inched along, Kenneth was stopping to introduce Ali to people and allow him to sign autographs. I figured that Ali and Kenneth may have known one another from Kenneth's days as a boxing promoter.

I decided to go downstairs and try to shake Ali's hand and, maybe, make him smile, recalling the days, five years before, in 1962, when I met Ali on the LA City College campus. One of Ali's high school buddies and I were friends at LACC, so thought I would ask Ali about our mutual friend, and maybe Kenneth would see me in a different light. Unfortunately, by the time I made my way downstairs to the first floor, Kenneth and Ali were leaving the Center in a limo.

Things never did get better between Kenneth and me, so three months after I came back to work, I transferred to another UPC on the near-West Side.

The work at the West Side Center was the same as that at the Center on the Southside, but I was much less familiar with the West Side schools and neighborhoods, so it took me a couple months to get comfortable. Also, my commute to the West Side from 92nd and Cottage Grove on the South Side was a lot longer.

Despite my lack of experience on the West Side (except for my time on "riot duty"), my transition to working with the NYC kids on the West Side was seamless. Most of the enrollees on the West Side were Black, with only a few Hispanics—we had a hand full of White enrollees in the program—but the challenges facing high school dropouts were the same, irrespective of race: boys drop out because they are disinterested and low achievers, or they are being affected by the increasing street gang activity, while most girls drop-out due to teen pregnancies.

Shortly after I started at the Center on the West Side, I came up with a program within the NYC Program called the "Job Orientation Program," which was designed to make the NYC enrollees more job ready. In this new program, when a kid enrolled in the NYC Program at any of the 9 Urban Progress Centers in Chicago, he or she would have to first complete two weeks in the Job Orientation Program before being assigned to a work site.

Initially, I chaired a committee of NYC professionals to brainstorm what the job orientation program would look like and how it would work. When the agency approved the concept, they found space for the program at a site just West of downtown.

Since I did not yet have a degree, the agency would not appoint me Director of the program; they appointed a brother named Futrell, who was a former high school Biology teacher, to be Director and made me Assistant Director.

In all, there were nine Urban Progress Centers located in some of Chicago's poor neighborhoods, and each Center had its own Neighborhood Youth Corps Program and staff. The staff from all nine Centers met together once per month, and in those meetings, we looked for suggestions and solutions to some of the challenges facing the NYC Program at each Center. One problem plaguing the NYC operations at several of the Centers mentioned was the matter of the NYC enrollees not being paid on time.

NYCs were classified as City of Chicago employees, and their paychecks should have been included with the paychecks being distributed to all City of Chicago employees who worked out of that Center, every two weeks. Often however, NYC's paychecks did not arrive at the Centers for distribution until the day after the regular payday, and sometimes, even the day after that.

Many of the NYC staff, especially if they were Black, wanted to dispel the myth held by many White people in the 60s that Black people would rather collect welfare than work for a living.

The staff argued that if people work and do not get paid on time, they should be expected to become demoralized and turn to a life of hustling to get money. I will never forget seeing a young Black man cry when his single mother of six accompanied him to the Center so that he could present her with his first, earned paycheck, and his check was not there. That was on a Thursday. The young man did not get his pay until Saturday.

NYC staff made several inquiries with the agency's management to find out why the enrollees checks were often late, only to be told that "the problem would be taken care of." When no reason for the late pay was ever given, the staff concluded that it was because management was indifferent. Finally, the NYC staff, me included, met with the Executive Director of the agency, Dr. Brooks, a small, Black man with a doctorate in Education from Columbia University.

—44—

"Listen Here"
Eddie Harris

    The meeting with Dr. Brooks, which lasted only about fifteen minutes, did not go well. He was dismissive and talked down to the committee. Following the short, unproductive meeting, the committee that met with Brooks voted to temporarily shut down NYC operations at their respective centers and meet downtown on the next day to picket agency headquarters. My activism juices were percolating, again. A few committee members volunteered to come up with picket signs.

    The strategy behind the committee's decision to shut down and walk out was based on estimating the effect that calling attention to thousands of disgruntled, mostly Black and Brown, teenagers, unsupervised in the streets, in the middle of a long, hot summer, would have on city officials, including Mayor Daley, who would be worried that tourists would get the impression that Chicago was unsafe. The committee hoped that Mayor Daley would order Brooks to fix the pay problem and get the NYC's and the staff who supervised them back to work.

    On the day of the walk-out, a Black woman from one of the Centers, whose husband was a news reporter for one of the major TV networks, told her husband about the walk-out, and he showed up outside the agency with a camera crew to begin broadcasting live from the picket line.

    In the meanwhile, Mayor Daley tried to tone down the public's concern by issuing a public statement on the news shows that read, "There is no cause for alarm. Those people who walked off their jobs are just clerks."

    When the reporter passed Daley's comment on to a "brother" on the picket line named Claude, Claude deftly peeled away from the picket line, and speaking into the reporter's microphone, he said, "Oh, Mayor Daley said that? Huh? Well, that just makes Mayor Daley the head clerk then, doesn't it?" A cheer went up from the picket line.

Twenty minutes into the demonstration, we got word that Dr. Brooks wanted to meet with the committee, again. No doubt, the TV coverage was making a difference in terms of public opinion. The walk-out strategy was working.

Brooks was as arrogant and condescending in the second meeting as he had been in the first meeting, trivializing the issue of late paychecks and repeating, "Everybody just calm down...these things have a way of working themselves out. Let's everybody go back to work. Don't worry, someone will get back to you—all of you."

Sensing the insincerity of Brooks, I called him out in the meeting for not showing leadership and taking the issue seriously. The meeting ended five minutes later, with Brooks promising to fix the problem.

The committee went back out to the picket line and held an impromptu meeting, telling troops to return to work, because Brooks had promised to fix the problem. As the picket line broke up, a "brother" from the committee whispered to me, "Man, that was beautiful the way you put Brooks in his place. I gotta start smokin whatever it is that you been smokin."

I knew that the "brother" called himself paying me a compliment because I was not afraid to speak out, but I did not like him thinking that my courage came from me smokin something.

For the two pay periods following that second meeting with Brooks, NYC paychecks arrived on time, with the rest of the paychecks, and I took satisfaction in knowing that I had a hand in convincing leadership of the agency to solve the problem. My satisfaction was short-lived, however.

One day, I was chatting with a senior executive at the agency, a Black man in his sixties named Lowe. Mr. Lowe had always been friendly toward me, once he found out that he had known my father since the 1940s. But in our conversation, Mr. Lowe scolded me about my behavior in the meeting with Dr. Brooks. He said that he wanted to remind me that the future leadership of Chicago comes from agencies like this.

I knew that Mr. Lowe felt that he was giving me sound advice, but what he was mostly doing was reminding me of why I hated Chicago politics. Less than a year after the flap over the NYC pay issues, I left the agency and the NYC Program—and the stench of

Chicago politics—with the help of a former White co-worker named Greg.

I always liked Greg, because he was feisty. He had a beard, before it was fashionable, and he was married to a dark-skinned Black woman with a close-cropped Afro. Greg and his wife had three young children. When I first met Greg, he held the same job as me as a Counselor in the NYC program, except that he worked at the Woodlawn Center, located in the middle of Blackstone Ranger gang territory.

When I visited the Woodlawn Center, one day, I was impressed with Greg's ability to be effective working with Black street gang members, without appearing to suck-up to them. By contrast, Greg's boss, who was a "brother," seemed much more inclined to pander to Blackstone Ranger leaders, who after eyeing me warily, offered me a swig from his bottle of orange soda. I declined their offer.

Greg left the agency a few months after the walkout, and for a while, I did not know where he was. Then I got a call from him, asking if I would be interested in working with him at the RCA Service Company television serviceman's apprenticeship program training site on the West Side. He told me that I would be doing the same kind of counseling work that I had been doing with NYC, but in RCA's pre-apprentice program, most of the enrollees would be adults.

The RCA Program appealed to me. The call from Greg could not have come at a better time. I interviewed with the Managing Director of the RCA Training Center, Greg's boss, and got the job.

—45—

"The Inflated Tear"
Rashann Roland Kirk

The RCA Program was exciting. The men were hired into the RCA program as paid apprentices. There were 45 men enrolled in the program, most of them Black, with two White men and two Hispanics. The men in the program ranged in age from 18 to 50. To me, the most intriguing thing about the RCA Program was that every man in the program had an opportunity to have a career as a certified television repairman and be gainfully employed, if not at the RCA Company, then at any number of electronic companies like Zenith or Westinghouse.

A man had to complete nine steps of an apprenticeship program to become a full-fledged TV repairman. Allowed to progress at their own rate, men finished the RCA program would be at Step 3 of the apprenticeship. I was excited about being in position to help adult men gain marketable skills and careers in a technical field.

There were three Counselors in the RCA Program: me, a "brother" named Eli, who, like me, Greg recruited from the NYC Program and Greg himself. We had caseloads of fifteen men, each. The RCA Program featured five White Technical Instructors who taught the program enrollees "basic electronics and how to troubleshoot and fix televisions. The RCA program also featured three Basic Education Teachers, all Black men, who taught Math, Communications and Customer Service. The team of Counselors, Technical Instructors and Basic Education Specialists provided the RCA Program enrollees with an immersive, supportive learning experience.

My daily commute to the RCA Training Center, where I was based, was about an hour, and I thought it might be a good time to move from my parents' house into my own apartment. As a Black Southsider, I viewed the West Side almost like another country and did not expect to find the type of housing opportunities I would be seeking.

One reason for my perception was that the West Side did not

have as large a Black middle-class as the Southside, nor did the West Side have many racially changing communities. Eventually, I found West Side communities like Austin, which were racially integrated, and I considered moving into an apartment in Austin. In the end though, I chickened out" and moved to an apartment on the South Side in Hyde Park, a community near the University of Chicago, which I knew well.

For the first six months of its operation, very few men dropped out of the RCA Program. We conducted exit interviews and learned that most of the men who left were seeking better paying jobs to support their families, or they had lost interest in becoming a television repairman.

A thirty-year old man in my caseload dropped out of the RCA Program to become a bus driver for the Chicago Transit Authority, for example. But most of the men who were there when I started were still in the program, six months later. They liked the Program, were satisfied with their progress, and a certain amount of camaraderie existed between the staff and the men in the Program.

In March of 1968, three of the younger men in the RCA Program approached Greg, Eli and me about helping them put on a mini-basketball tournament between four teams that the men had organized, and we agreed to do it. The men had already arranged to play the tournament games at the Navy Pier Gym, which was being run by the Chicago Fire Department, since the University of Illinois at Chicago had moved to the Circle Campus.

One of the tournament games was on a Thursday afternoon in April 1968, and I refereed the game. I had not been inside the Navy Pier Gym since 1965, so I was impressed by the diverse group of hundreds of men and women using the gym in activities ranging from basketball to gymnastics to volleyball.

During a time-out in the game I was refereeing, I noticed a tall, middle-aged Black man, dressed in street clothes, silhouetted in the entrance to the gym like an apparition, waving and shouting at me. The gym was so noisy that I could not hear what the man was saying, so I walked a few feet in his direction, cupping my ear to signal that I needed him to speak louder.

The man took one step into the cavernous gym, and in a loud voice, he said, "You people *do* know that Dr. Martin Luther King was shot and killed, today, don't you?"

All activity in the gym stopped, as if in suspended animation. No one— Black, White, Asian, Hispanic or other said anything for the next several seconds, except for a woman who squeaked, "Oh, my God!" As the gym began to come back to life, several people ran towards the exits, while others stood, talking quietly.

One of the RCA brothers stood, holding the basketball against his hip and pleaded, "Come on y'all, can we finish the game?" No one answered him. At that moment, I did not consider Dr. King's legacy. What did cross my mind though, was that Chicago was in line for another race riot.

When I finished my six months active duty in the Army back in 1968, my Military Occupational Status (MOS) was changed from Infantry to Military Police and my base Armory was changed from the Armory at 52nd and Cottage Grove to the Chicago Avenue Armory on the Lakefront in Lincoln Park.

The Navy Pier gym was practically across the street from the Chicago Avenue Armory, so I wrestled with whether I should drive home to my apartment in Hyde Park and wait for the National Guard to call me, or if just go directly to the Chicago Avenue Armory. I opted to go home and pack toiletries, etc., since there was no way of predicting how long I would be living in the Armory, during riot duty.

As I drove South down Lake Shore Drive on my way to Hyde Park, I could see what I suspected was smoke from arson fires in the distance. The rioting had already begun. That King's murder led to rioting came as no surprise to anyone Black. After all, King himself had reminded America how rioting was the voice of the voiceless.

What bothered me about rioting, however, was the probability that once again Black people would be burning down their own neighborhoods and victimizing the Black people living in those neighborhoods, including people who were not rioting and looting— people like the "brothers" in the RCA Program who were trying to better themselves by going to school or getting a better job, or people wanting to go to church or people wanting to shop for groceries. Once again, I pondered the role of Black National Guardsmen.

Given the extent to which Dr. King has been lionized in the last 50 years, having streets named for him, statues— even having a

National holiday named for him, it may be hard to understand that in 1968, not all Black people viewed King as a hero, with his preachy style, *We Shall Overcome* attitude and nonviolent martyrdom.

There were a lot of Black people, like me, who felt that the time had come in America for Black people to use *any means necessary* to attain racial justice, to include rioting. However, while Dr. King's effectiveness was a matter of debate, within the Black community, his murder by a White, ex-con and avowed segregationist, pissed-off all Black people.

—46—

"We're A Winner"
The Impressions

As anticipated, the call-up from the National Guard came shortly after I got to my apartment. Hastily, I changed into my fatigues, gathered some gear and threw it into a duffel bag, and then I sped north on Lake Shore Drive to the Chicago Avenue Armory. I pulled into the parking lot at the same time as a Black soldier in my platoon named Everett.

He and I walked into the Armory together as I complained about being called-up for riot duty so soon after having just returned from six months of active duty in the Army. Everett talked about riots hurting and inconveniencing "Black folks in the community," and when I told him that I had been thinking about how Black Guardsman can better serve Black people who are trapped in riot-torn neighborhoods, he said, "Yeah, wonder what we could do?"

Everett and I were both National Guard veterans. Everett was still a Private while I had attained the rank of Specialist. We had been in the Guard for two years, fulfilled our six months in the Army obligation and seen action in two race riots. And even though our MOS had been changed from "Infantry" to "Military Police," we were on the verge of being deployed for riot duty in the same fashion as always, with rifles, bayonets, bullets and protective masks. Everett and I wanted to be a part of something different.

The first minutes of a riot duty deployment is a hectic time in an armory, with hundreds of men, outfitted in gear, lining up and boarding the trucks and jeeps that will take them into the streets. That activity in the armory makes it easy to hide in plain sight, if you are so inclined, and that is exactly what Everett and I managed to do.

When I was first assigned to the Chicago Avenue Armory, I was promoted to Specialist as a result of being assigned to the Administrative Office in the Armory, and, as a Specialist, I had clearance to be able to take a Jeep assigned to the Administrative Office out of the Motor Pool, so Everett and I grabbed a radio and we drove a Jeep out of the Motor Pool and out of the Armory and followed the convoy.

Once we were out the Armory and driving down streets, I was careful to stay far enough behind the convoy to avoid being spotted. Everett and I heard a radio transmission indicating that National Guard units were being ordered West on Chicago Avenue to the all-Black, Cabrini-Green Public Housing Project, so that was where Everett and I decided to go.

As we got close to the Cabrini-Green Project high-rise buildings, we saw National Guard troops and Chicago policemen, running with weapons drawn. I pulled the Jeep to the side and let some National Guardsmen and Chicago policeman run past with their guns drawn. I asked a Black policeman what was going on, and he answered, out of breath, "We think we've located that sniper who has been shooting at the Fire Station and preventing fire trucks from leaving the Station to fight fires."

As the policeman ran ahead, two chatty Black women hurried down the sidewalk on the heels of the policemen, and I heard one of them say, "Yeah, y'all go on ahead and get whoever's keeping firemen from putting-out fires. These fools out here rioting been shooting and looting and setting fires to stores... and now people ain't got nowhere to get no food. My babies got to have food... and milk!" The other woman laughed, "Girl, I know that's rightl!"

That is when I told Everett my idea.

During the 1966 West Side Riot, my National Guard Battalion lived in the Armory for a week. That meant that the Mess Hall in the Armory was continuously preparing meals for Guardsmen as they moved in and out of the Armory.

A lot of the food that was cooked, however, was never eaten and got thrown away, since the Army does not serve the soldiers leftovers. My idea was to see if the Mess Sergeant, a large Black man named Perkins, would allow me and Everett take uneaten food out of the Armory and donate the food to food kitchens in riot-torn neighborhoods. Everett loved my idea, so we turned the Jeep around and headed back to the Armory to see Sergeant Perkins.

Sergeant Perkins's crew was busy in kitchen in the Armory,

cleaning up after supper, when I approached him about taking uneaten food out of the Armory instead of throwing it away, and donating it to food kitchens. Sergeant Perkins said he did not care if we took food that would otherwise be thrown away, "as long as you bring back my pots and pans."

Perkins showed Everett and me where the uneaten food was stacked, still in serving pans, waiting to be thrown away. He never asked us if we had any authorization or orders to do what we were about to do.

With stacks of food in sight, Everett and I realized that our plan had a chance to work. We grabbed as many of the pans of fried chicken, green beans and macaroni and cheese that we could fit in the Jeep. We laid our rifles on the floor of the Jeep behind the front seats, and we covered them with a poncho and stacked the serving pans, full of food, on top of the poncho, and we covered the pans of food under another poncho, so Everett and I drove out of the Armory with the food and headed back to the Cabrini-Green neighborhood.

Driving slowly down the dark streets around Cabrini-Green, we saw a small group of Black men and women standing and talking, outside a brick church on Elm Street. When I pulled over, a pleasant-looking man walked to the Jeep and introduced himself as pastor of the church. As I was telling the pastor about the food we wanted to donate, Everett lifted the poncho to show the pastor the pans of food.

Smiling, the pastor said that his church had a food kitchen and would put the food to good use. Then he called for three young men to take food out of the Jeep and into the church.

The next day, Everett and I went back to the church and collected Sergeant Perkin's pots and pans. When I gave them back to Sergeant Perkins, he grinned and said, "We're cooking pork chops tonight, if you're interested." Everett and I worked our plan one more night. It was satisfying.

—47—
"It's A Beautiful Morning"
The Rascals

The rest of the King riots were the usual, as race riots went, with unorganized looting of mostly-White-owned stores in Black neighborhoods. When the four days of rioting ended, I went back to my job at RCA. Joking with a couple brothers in my caseload, I told them that I had seen them looting while patrolling the streets with my National Guard unit. Both men laughed, and one of them said, "Naw, man, you didn't see me. No lawd! You mighta seen my wife lootin, but I had to stay home with the kids!"

By summer, things had quieted down in Chicago. I was optimistic that they would stay that way, and I would not be interrupted again for riot duty. But social unrest was growing in America, due to the growing anti-war sentiment over the ongoing war in Vietnam.

Popular Massachusetts Senator Bobby Kennedy, the brother of assassinated President John F. Kennedy, was himself shot and killed in June of 1968, leaving the National Democratic Party without the candidate for President who many had hoped would succeed President Lyndon Johnson, who declared he was not running for re-election.

Vice President, Johnson had succeeded President Kennedy, in 1963, when Kennedy was assassinated, and had served as President since. Johnson was not a popular President because of his failure to end the war in Viet Nam. The "whole world watched" to see who would emerge from the Democratic Convention in August of 1968, as the candidate for President who would run against Republican nominee, Richard M. Nixon.

With the Democratic National Party's Convention being held in Chicago, the party's headquarters was set up at the Conrad Hilton Hotel on Michigan Avenue, across from Grant Park. Anti-war demonstrators wasted no time having their voices heard in Grant Park during the Convention, which ran from August 26-August 29. The statue of Civil War Union General John Logan that stands prominently in Grant Park became the rallying place for the anti-War demonstrators, the vast majority of whom were White people. Demonstrations at the General Logan statue grew larger and more violent during the Convention, and at times the demonstrators nearly overwhelmed the Chicago Police. So once again, my National Guard unit was called up.

*****

When I was a little boy, my parents brought my sister and me downtown to the statue of General Logan, where my sister and I would run up the hill to the base of the statue, and then roll back down to the bottom of the hill, just to it all over again, until we got tired, or until Mom and Dad got tired of watching us.

Going to the hill ranks high among my most cherished childhood experiences. So, when I saw those violent, anti-War demonstrations taking place on my beloved hill, I had mixed emotions. On the one hand, I empathized with the "peaceniks" demonstrating against the unpopular war and being brutalized by the Chicago police, while, on the other hand, I hated to see the grungy, dope-smoking demonstrators desecrating my hill.

At times, there were thousands of anti-war demonstrators in Grant Park at the statue of General Logan but the real rioters were the Chicago police. In fact, Chicago Police's heavy-handed, nearly out-of-control behavior became a national story, and the Chicago police were nationally criticized. From the floor of the Democratic Convention, Chicago Mayor Daley, who was prone to misspeak, tried to defend the Chicago police on national television by saying, "The Chicago Police are not there to create disorder, the Police are there to preserve disorder!!"

*****

When I reported to the Armory for the call-up during the Convention, I went directly to the Administration office and began filing records. I ended up working in the office, and well into the night. Around 11p.m., I saw two MPs, one White and one Black, as they escorted a White Chicago policeman into the Armory. Since the policeman's holster was empty. I asked the White MP what was going on and he told me that the policeman was "using so much force and was so out of control that we had to disarm him to keep him from killing somebody." Later that night, the policeman and his firearm were released to the custody of his District Commander.

After seeing that Chicago policeman restrained, I wanted to get out to The Hill to see the action for myself. The next morning, I took a Jeep to Grant Park, but when I got to The Hill, things were quiet at the Statue of General Logan, although hundreds of demonstrators were still milling about. The National Guard had formed a buffer zone between the police and the demonstrators, and some of the demonstrators were placing flowers into the barrels of the Guardsmen's rifles, showing their appreciation for the protection from the overzealous policemen that the Guard had provided. It was a heartwarming but bizarre scene.

One part of me was sorry that I had not been directly involved in restoring order on my beloved hill, while on the other hand, I was glad to have avoided all the turmoil. The call-up for the demonstrations in Grant Park during the 1968 Democratic Conventions was the last time I was activated for riot duty as a member of the National Guard.

—48—

"Beginnings"
Chicago Transit Authority

Tom Paulick and I became friends in 1966, when I was working in the NYC Program, and Tom was part of the team that came to the Center to audit the program. Tom and I got the chance to talk a lot during the audit, and I liked him. Before joining the agency, Tom had served in the Peace Corps in Chile, and I enjoyed hearing about his experiences. Tom was a Notre Dame alum, and he and I also enjoyed talking college football. He invited me to go to a Notre Dame football game with him in South Bend, Indiana, and our friendship grew from there.

While I was away at six months, Tom left the agency and took a position in corporate America as the Recruiting Manager at a firm that produced Armour Meats and Dial Soap, called Armour-Dial. When I got back from six months, Tom and I resumed our friendship, and in the fall of 1968, he asked me if I would be interested in working with him recruiting grocery products salesmen and saleswomen. I reminded Tom that I was hours short of completing my degree, but he assured me that would not pose a problem if I was in school and committed to finishing my degree. Tom told me he was confident that I had the requisite skills to be a good college recruiter.

I regarded a move into corporate America as an extraordinary opportunity for someone like me, who was Black and had not finished college. I had grown tired of working in job training programs, while at the same time, corporate America had started to hire Blacks. My buddies, Rusty and Adams, had each landed excellent jobs at Johnson & Johnson, after completing their degrees at the University of Illinois at Champaign, and I felt that I could follow in their footsteps.

Although Tom never used the term, affirmative action, relative to my being hired at Armour-Dial, that is what it was, I suppose. In the on-going national debate concerning the fairness and efficacy of affirmative action that began in the 60s, some people opposed affirmative action programs because they perceived it as enabling minorities to get jobs where they were not qualified, jobs that should have gone to a qualified White person.

Some White people could not conceive that a Black person without degree could possibly be as qualified for a corporate job as a White person *with* a degree. But it was Tom who pointed out to me that how, in my previous jobs with the agency as well as with RCA, I had successfully interviewed and selected scores of people. Tom pointed out to me that affirmative action meant providing opportunities for minorities and other protected classes who had the ability to do a job, but had been systematically overlooked. I fit that profile.

To get the College Recruiter position at Armour-Dial, I had to interview with Tom's boss and Tom's boss's boss. Armour-Dial's corporate offices were downtown at Wacker Drive and Michigan Avenue, close by the Chicago River, and on the day of my interviews, Tom's assistant, a young, Black woman named Sylvia met me in the lobby and told me that she would escort me to both my interviews and answer any questions I might have about the company.

Then she volunteered, "Tom's boss, Bill, is a good guy. I think you will like him. But Vince, the VP of HR— I am not so sure about him," she laughed. "I don't know how he really feels about Black people, and we could definitely use more Black people around here."

She went on to explain that out of 1,000 employees, Armour-Dial had only two Black professionals, a Chemist and a Transportation & Distribution Analyst. If I got the job, I would be the third. Sylvia proved to be right about my interviews. I came away from my interview with Bill, Tom's boss, feeling good. Bill had been warm and friendly and asked thoughtful questions, such as, "What do you think your biggest adjustments will be in moving from a social services agency into corporate America?"

I enjoyed having to consider answers to those kinds of questions. Bill also asked me what I had learned from working with high school dropouts, which gave me a chance to tell him that I had learned that many high school dropouts were often bright, but they were victims of their environments. Bill smiled and nodded at my answers. I felt that I had made a favorable impression on him.

Vince proved harder to read, as Sylvia had predicted. He was patronizing as he started the interview with small talk, saying, "I'm guessing you grew up on the Southside, so I'll bet you're a White Sox fan?" I just smiled, preferring not to explain to him how a Black Southsider like me became a Cub's fan.

Then Vince got into the interview by asking, "George, how do you feel about civil rights?" I did not want to say anything that might reflect poorly on Tom's judgment in recommending me for the job, so I think I told Vince something like, "It's sad that the fair and just treatment of people of color still needs special legislation 100 years after the Civil War." Vince stared at me, but he did not say anything.

The interview with Vince was uncomfortable, tense and short. When I left his office, I had no idea how I had impressed him, one way or the other. But that evening, Tom called and congratulated me. I was Armour-Dial's new College Recruiter. I was elated.

As soon as I got to work the next day, I told Greg that I would be leaving RCA to take a job as a College Recruiter for Armour-Dial. Greg smiled, shook my hand and congratulated me. Then he told me that he was also leaving RCA, moving to South Carolina to join the faculty of a small, private liberal arts college.

I thought about Greg with his Black wife and mixed children and what life could be like for them in the land of staunch segregationist Republican Senator Strom Thurmond. Yet if anyone could handle such an environment, it would be Greg.

—49—

"Shopping for Clothes"
The Coasters

As soon as I learned I had landed the job at Armour-Dial, I realized that since I would be working in corporate America, I would need a new wardrobe. In my previous jobs, I had been able to get away wearing sweaters and going tie-less. Not being a church-goer, I owned one slightly out-of-date suit, meaning I would have to build a wardrobe from scratch. I looked through the consignment inventory in my father's shop, but I could not find anything. Dad offered to make a couple suits for me, but I told him to hold off until I had a chance to shop around downtown.

It was June when I started at Armour-Dial, and I used my newly-acquired American Express Card to buy two summer-weight suits, including a light-blue seersucker suit, three dress shirts and three ties. Those two summer suits were my first-ever, store-bought suits.

I felt good about my purchases until the bill from American Express came in the mail. Somehow, I missed the fine print that required I pay in-full. Once I paid American Express, I was not left with enough cash to park downtown and go to lunch at any of Chicago's great, downtown restaurants. But I was lookin sharp!

My first on-campus recruiting visit was not scheduled until January 1970. The schedule had been set-up by the Administrative Assistant, Donna, who I inherited from the previous recruiter. However, on the day that I started at Armour-Dial, there was a resume on my desk from a recent graduate of Loras College in Iowa whose name was Greg Gumbel.

Back in 1965, when I volunteered to serve on a Community Advisory Committee, I often sat next to a Judge named Richard Gumbel, who always encouraged me to "speak up, let people know what you are thinking… Don't let these old codgers like these Aldermen intimidate you." When I saw the name "Gumbel" on the resume, I was eager to find out if Greg was related to Judge

Gumbel, so I called Greg in for an interview.

Greg did in fact turn out to be Judge Gumbel's son. Greg was thoughtful and articulate, and I was impressed enough to forward his resume to Armour-Dial's Midwest Regional Sales Manager to be considered for hire. But when I called Greg that evening to schedule the interview with the Sales Manager, I got a response from Greg that I had not expected.

He told me he had been thinking about the sales job we had discussed in our interview, but he was not interested in the job. My first reaction was disappointment that I would not be able to impress my bosses at Armour-Dial with my first successful recruit. My second thought was that Greg was making a career mistake if he turned down an opportunity to get a job in corporate America. However, I could not think of a way to have that discussion with Greg.

I was humbled by the reality that I had been unable to get a "brother" interested in taking advantage of the chance to get into corporate America. Then again, how could I have known that Greg would end up being a popular, well-known American television sportscaster and the first Black announcer to call play-by-play for a major sports championship in the United States, when he announced Super Bowl XXXV in 2001?

Me wearing my first, store-bought suit, in my first job in corporate America at Armour-Dial, Inc., in 1969.

—50—

"Is It Because I'm Black"
Syl Johnson

Before I visited any campuses, I spent time in Cleveland, Ohio, with a White Sales Manager named Don, who I learned had been my predecessor as Armour-Dial's College Recruiter. Don and I talked in detail about traits to look and probe for when trying to determine if a candidate would be a good, Grocery Products salesperson.

Don and I went into several stores so I could observe and familiarize myself with a salesperson's job, and by the time that I left Cleveland, I knew the job well enough to start screening college grads. When Don dropped me at the airport for my flight back to Chicago, his last words to me were, "I hope you have more success recruiting Blacks than I did."

I wanted to scream to Don that I had not been hired to only recruit Black people, but I knew that many White people are incredulous when it comes to the idea that a Black person can or should be allowed to assess a White person. I chalked Don's remarks up to his lack of sophistication.

In December 1969, a month before my first, scheduled college recruiting trip, Fred Hampton, the popular leader of Chicago's Black Panther Party, was shot and killed during a pre-dawn raid by agents of the Cook County State's Attorney's Office. Hampton was a "social revolutionary" who the FBI and Cook County State's Attorney Ed Hanrahan suspected of posing a radical threat to society, despite Hampton's success at establishing a "rainbow coalition" in Chicago that brought together Black, White and Hispanic street gangs.

Although I did not know Hampton personally, I knew people who did, and they all had good things to say about Hampton. At first, I worried that Hampton's death might lead to more race riots, and my National Guard unit would be activated, but I need not have worried, since nobody rioted in Chicago in the Winter.

Hampton's murder made me feel conflicted, as I was about to

embark on my first college recruiting trip, in January. I questioned whether I should be struttin my stuff in airports, across the country, as though there was no race problem in America, or if I should I be laying low and preparing to take to the streets to protest the systemic racism that continued to result in the slaughter of Black leaders.

It was a reminder of how schizophrenic race can make Black professionals feel. Adding to my paranoia was the fact that my first campus recruiting trip was going to be Tallahassee, Florida— the South— where I would be recruiting at Florida State University (FSU) and Florida A&M University (FAMU). I had never been in the South before, and with race being in the news so much, I was a little nervous.

—51—

"Blasé"
Archie Shepp

Donna, the Administrative Assistant I inherited, was a bright and delightful young woman of Lebanese descent. She had done a great job of getting me ready for my first recruiting trip and made helpful introductions to Placement Office leadership at both FSU and FAMU. Donna had developed an especially good relationship with the Placement Director at FSU, a White guy named Stan, and she promised that my experience at FSU would be good.

Stan was a small, nattily dressed man in his 50s who greeted me as he would an old friend. He was also a huge college basketball fan, which turned out to be a good segue as he and I got to know each other. Stan invited me to ride with him and his wife to Jacksonville University to watch Florida State play a game.

The most remarkable thing about the trip to Jacksonville was Stan, pointing out the commercial properties and malls he had developed in a previous life, as he described it. Stan told me that he had once had millions, but he lost his fortune when he divorced his first wife.

My first recruiting trip was a success. I ended up referring two White kids from FSU who Armour-Dial subsequently hired in Orlando and Fort Lauderdale, and one Black kid from FAMU, who Armour-Dial hired in Philadelphia, his hometown.

The worst part of my first recruiting trip was that I traveled with only a raincoat, because nobody warned me that it gets cold in Tallahassee in January. For the rest of the winter and spring, I recruited at ten more colleges, including The University of Southern California, the University of Wisconsin, Southern Illinois University, DePaul and Loyola Universities in Chicago, among others.

In the spring, Donna informed me that she had successfully made a bid for a Marketing Associate position in Armour-Dial's Marketing Department and would be leaving the College Recruiting Department in May. I was happy for Donna, because I learned that she had majored in Marketing at Marquette University and had been looking for a chance to get into a Marketing job. Donna's leaving the College Recruiting Department meant that I needed to find a new Assistant.

Donna assured me that she would help me find her replacement, even if it meant helping me after she started her new job. She started screening candidates right away. I told her to be sure to include some Black candidates, and she did. After a couple weeks of searching, Donna came up with three candidates for me to interview. Two of the candidates Donna brought were bright and experienced young Black women. I was not impressed with one of the Black candidate's work experience, and yet the other Black candidate was asking for more money than I wanted to pay.

I ended up hiring the third candidate that Donna presented, a blonde White woman named Barbara who, like Donna, was a Marquette University graduate. I had not noticed that Barbara was attractive until I noticed a bunch of different White guys, who I had never seen around the office before, walking slowly past my office to catch a glimpse of Barbara while I was interviewing her. Admittedly, Barbara's attractiveness briefly gave me pause, but I hired her anyway, and she hit the ground running.

Barbara was single and lived downtown, and she was often the first one into the office in the morning. So when I got to the office, one morning and Barbara was not there, I was not sure what to expect. Thirty minutes passed and Barbara had neither come in or called, so I began wonder if Barbara had mentioned that she would not be in and I had forgotten or if I had overlooked a message that she may have left me.

I began poking around Barbara's desk and looking through the calendar on her desk, and that is where I finally saw an envelope addressed to me that was sticking out between the pages on the calendar. I opened the envelope and read the note and laughed out loud: Barbara and her boyfriend had eloped and were on their way to live in Colorado. I was back to needing an Assistant.

—52—
"Everywhere"
Fleetwood Mac

When I told Donna that Barbara had resigned and eloped, she looked deflated. Then Donna assured me that she would not leave me hanging and would stay involved with the search for Barbara's replacement. In the meanwhile, I had one more recruiting trip on my schedule to Michigan State University in East Lansing, Michigan, a trip I had circled on my calendar because my friend, Bo Rogers, was a student there.

Bo had played football at Michigan State when he first got out of high school in 1962. He then left MSU, got drafted into the Army, did a tour in Vietnam, came back and re-enrolled at MSU. I had recently seen Bo at a Christmas party and told him that I would be recruiting at Michigan State in spring, Bo said he would meet me in MSU's Placement Center, and he did. When I walked into the MSU's Placement Center in April 1970, Bo was there to greet me with his toothy grin and slightly crossed eyes.

Before I set up to start interviewing students, Bo told me to come with him, because he wanted me to meet someone. I followed Bo into a small office where a tall, well-built, good-looking Black man was standing behind his desk and grinning broadly.

The man was Gene Washington, the star wide receiver for the Minnesota Vikings, who had at one time had been Bo's teammate when they played football at Michigan State together. In 1970, National Football League players were not making mega-bucks like they do today, and many of them like Gene had offseason jobs. Working in MSU's Placement Center was Gene's offseason job.

When Bo told Gene that I was a Chicago Bears fan, Gene said, "Well then, there is somebody else you should meet before you start your interviews today."

Gene got up and led Bo and me to a large room where other corporate recruiters were preparing to start their interviews. Gene came up behind a large Black man whose back was to us and tapped him on the shoulder. When the large man saw that it was Gene, he stood up and they heartily shook hands. Gene introduced me and Bo to the big man who was Bob Pickens, an offensive tackle with the Chicago Bears.

Bob was a mountain of man, standing six-feet-four inches tall and weighing well over 300 pounds. He had been the first American to compete in Greco-Roman wrestling in the Olympics in 1964 before being drafted by the Chicago Bears. Bob's offseason job, it turns out, was recruiting for Xerox.

When Bo left to attend his class and Gene went back to his office, Bob and I chatted for a few minutes before we each had to start our interviews, and we discovered that our offices in Chicago were practically across the street from each other, so we planned to have lunch together when we got back to Chicago.

A week later, Bob and I met for lunch at a restaurant on Michigan Avenue that was a short walk from our offices. I told him that I had recently lost my Administrative Assistant and was looking to hire a new one, preferably Black. Bob laughed and said that he was in the process of looking for an assistant too. We each described the type of experience and skill level we were looking for in an assistant and how much we were looking to pay.

At one point, Bob said, "I'll tell you what: when I'm interviewing candidates, if I see somebody who I think you'd like, and I'll send that person across the street to you. And if you see somebody who you think I might like, send that person over here to me." Bob and I laughed and shook hands.

A week later, Bob called me and said that he was interviewing a "sister" in his office who he thought I might like. He said that the young lady he was interviewing was good, but he had already committed to hiring someone else. So I said, "Okay, send her over, and I'll interview her."

I was impressed with everything about Gloria as soon as I laid eyes on her and her warm smile. Gloria's Afro was beautiful, and I got a kick out of watching her twist and contort her body so that a White woman could not touch her Afro to see how it felt. Gloria was a senior at Loyola University, majoring in Education.

Her home was Canton, Mississippi, but she was living with an older sister and her family in South Shore. Gloria was self-effacing, bright and serious, and at the end of our interview, I offered her the Assistant's job, and she accepted.

From the start, I could tell that there was something special about Gloria. She was kind, thoughtful and authentic and, from the start, I liked being around her.

A dear friend who has always believed in me, Tom Paulick.

—53—

"Thank You (Falettinme Be Mice Elf Agin)"
Sly and the Family Stone

South Shore is a short ride from Hyde Park, where I lived, so a few weeks after she started at Armour-Dial, I began driving Gloria to her sister's house in South Shore after work. The more I looked forward to driving Gloria home, the more that I knew that I wanted to build a relationship with her.

At the time, I was not in a serious relationship with anyone, and as I learned, neither was Gloria. Finally, I got up enough nerve to ask her out on a date. Intra-office romances were not expressly forbidden at Armour-Dial, but I was not sure how it would be viewed if someone were to see Gloria and I out together outside of work, so I tried to be discreet.

In July, Sly and the Family Stone, one of my favorite R&B/funk bands, was slated to do a free concert at the Band Shell in Grant Park, starting around 6 p.m., right after work. So I took a deep breath and asked Gloria if she would like to go to the concert with me, and she said she would.

To avoid arousing suspicion in case we were spotted by someone from Armour-Dial, Gloria and I agreed that we would leave the office separately and meet in the park. Grant Park is about a mile from the Armour-Dial offices, and Gloria left the office first, while I followed fifteen minutes later.

Gloria rode a bus to Grant Park from the office, but I got my car out of the garage, drove it to Grant Park, and I found a place to park not too far from the Band Shell. I jumped out of my car and hurried into the park to find Gloria.

The concert had not started, but the Park was rapidly filling up with people, and the reefer smoke in the air was getting thicker. The racially-mixed crowd was soon revved up, and I began to worry that I might not find Gloria in the turmoil I was sure would soon follow.

When a helicopter hovered just above the tree line, the crowd began to buzz. A woman standing near me shouted that she could see *Sly, in the cockpit, next to the pilot!* A cheer went up from the crowd, which began running around, as if trying to figure out where the helicopter would land and forming a circle.

I hung back on the edge of the crowd, still searching for Gloria, when suddenly the helicopter stopped descending and ascended with a whoosh, creating an updraft in the muggy air. A collective gasp arose from the frenzied crowd as the helicopter continued climbing until it was well above the tree-line.

Then, the helicopter banked sharply and headed south and east out over Lake Michigan. Realizing that the helicopter purportedly carrying Sly was leaving Grant Park, the crowd erupted into a riot, with beer bottles and other objects flying through the air.

I looked for a place to avoid being trampled by the rampaging crowd, and that was when I spotted Gloria, looking *as cool as the other side of the pillow* to quote the late ESPN broadcaster, Stuart Scott. Gloria saw me making my way towards, her and she began running to meet me. Holding hands, we ran to my car, promising each other that our next date would be better.

—54—

"Too Late to Turn Back Now"
Cornelius Brothers and Sister Rose

After escaping the riot in Grant Park, Gloria and I continued to date, caring less and less about who saw us. We went to live concerts, movies, museums and picnics and we took walks together. Gloria and I double-dated with my old Army buddy, Jimmy, and his wife, Mildred, a few times and Jimmy told me that he "figured Gloria must be 'the one' because she's the only lady we've ever seen you take out more than once." Jimmy was prescient.

In August 1970, my National Guard unit went to Camp McCoy, Wisconsin, for the Guard's annual two-week encampment. Since I had been in the Guard for a few years, they permitted me to drive my own car the 250 miles to Camp McCoy instead of riding in the convoy. Having my own car made it possible for me to drive back to Chicago to spend the weekend with Gloria, so as soon as we were dismissed on Saturday afternoon, I jumped in my car and sped to Chicago.

Gloria was both surprised and happy to see me. It was a special moment for both of us— one that neither of us has ever forgotten. Gloria and I dated for the rest of the summer. In September, Gloria resigned from Armour-Dial so that she could complete her last semester of college. On Gloria's last day at Armour-Dial, I let Tom know that Gloria and I had "something special going." He smiled, shook my hand and said, "She's terrific. Congratulations."

I happily faced the reality that Gloria was the person I wanted to be with for the rest of my life. In November, Gloria's father came to Chicago for the wedding, and Reverend Ammons married Gloria and me. We are still together.

In January of 1971, Armour-Dial announced that it had been acquired by the Greyhound Corporation and was moving its corporate offices to Phoenix, Arizona. The newly formed firm of Greyhound-Armour, Inc. offered me my same position in Phoenix, so Gloria and I gave the move to Phoenix serious consideration. She and I went on a house-hunting visit to Phoenix, provided by Armour-Dial, riding around Phoenix with a realtor for two days, looking at houses and neighborhoods.

We saw some great-looking properties, but Gloria was unsettled by the relative lack of greenery implied in the concept of desert landscaping, and neither of us were comfortable with the fact that we did not know any Black people in Phoenix. Also, Phoenix was too far away from our families in Chicago and Canton, Mississippi, so we passed on the move, and I started looking for another job.

*****

In the early 1970s, a handful of major corporations had learned how to mine the rich veins of diverse talent that corporate America had overlooked for years. Armour-Dial had just begun to move toward affirmative action when they hired me in 1969. Firms like Johnson & Johnson (J&J), on the other hand, where my buddy, Rusty, was a Production Engineer Manager, had been hiring Blacks into management positions for years.

J&J was so far out in front of most corporations in terms of hiring Blacks into management positions that the Chicago plant where Band-Aids were made published an ad, showing photos of every Black man and woman in management. When I told Rusty that I was leaving Armour-Dial and needed to find another job, he urged me to pursue opportunities at J&J.

Rusty immediately hooked me up with a headhunter named Sandy, a "sister" he met in graduate school at Northwestern University. 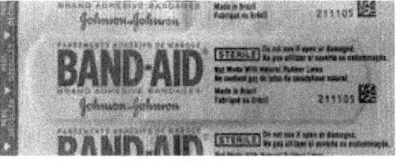 Sandy got me an interview at J&J's Midwest Surgical Dressings Plant (where Band-Aids are made) at 65th and Cicero in Chicago, near Midway Airport.

J&J hired me as Manager of Wage and Salary and Benefits Administration, in a plant of nearly 3000 employees, including 2500 hourly employees, represented by the Amalgamated Clothing and Textile Workers Union. I had landed a great job at an excellent company.

—55—

"Just My Imagination"
The Temptations

Gloria's brother, Ricky and our first born, Marcus. Ricky came from Mississippi and lived with us in Chicago, thru high school and college at the University of Notre Dame.

In the Spring of 1971, Gloria and I drove to her home in Canton, Mississippi. It was my first trip to the State of Mississippi, which as far as Black people were concerned, had its own mythology. Many of my Black friends imagined Mississippi as the most dangerous place in America for Black people, overrun with active Ku Klux Klansmen and White Citizens Council bigots, routinely lynching Black folks, with impunity, like they did Emmett Till.

My heart was in my throat from the moment we entered the State of Mississippi, on Interstate 55. I recoiled when we drove across a bridge over the Tallahatchie River, the River in which Emmett Till's body was thrown into by the White men who lynched him in 1955. Gloria, of course, was aware of Mississippi's awful history, but she assured me that I "should be fine, as long as you stay around your own people and mind your own business."

Gloria's parents had raised eleven children, but only one of them still lived at home in Mississippi— her youngest brother, Ricky. Ricky was 14 and very bright. He was an impressive young man who was curious, serious and always eager to be helpful. He had completed his first year of high school at a Catholic School in Canton, from which Gloria and each one of her five sisters had graduated. I felt that a bright kid like Ricky might benefit from being in Chicago, which offered more educational opportunities. Evidently Gloria and her mother felt the same way, and Ricky came to Chicago to live with Gloria and me.

With Ricky joining us, Gloria and I moved to a larger apartment in Hyde Park. Ricky attended Kenwood Public High School, an integrated school, a short walk from our apartment. In the meanwhile, I finished college with a BS Degree in Economics from the Illinois Institute of Technology.

—56—

"What's Going On"
Marvin Gaye

J & J's Surgical Dressings Plant was only a few miles from the place where I came close to having to use force against those White men who threatened me when I was in the National Guard and on riot duty in Cicero, in 1966. By 1971, race relations in America were in a somewhat different place from where they were in 1966, but the iconic voices of Malcolm X and Martin Luther King that inspired my generation had been stilled by assassins' bullets.

Meanwhile, the Civil Rights Act was the law of the land, addressing discrimination in employment which, had given birth to the Equal Employment Opportunity Commission, the EEOC, which had the power to adjudicate in cases involving racial discrimination in employment.

J&J's plant was close to several all-White communities that had long histories of racial animus, and many of J&J's White, hourly employees lived in those communities. So I anticipated that race relations could be sitting on a powder keg at J&J, despite the company's commendable affirmative action initiatives. I did not see many signs of race issues in the plant, probably because J&J was one of the first large firms to establish the position of "Manager of Diversity and Inclusion."

As Wage and Salary and Benefits Administrator, I reported to the Director of Human Resources, a White guy named Larry, who described himself to me as a White liberal. Larry invited Gloria and me to spend a Saturday afternoon with his wife and four little girls at their home in Elmhurst, a well-heeled suburb, west of Chicago.

Gloria and I were not excited about using up our Saturday to drive out to Elmhurst, but wanting to get off to a good start with my boss, we accepted his invitation. We even brought along our niece, Kim, at Larry's insistence, since Kim was around the age of Larry's daughters. A nice time was had by all.

The following Monday at the plant, I told Rusty that Gloria and I had visited Larry and his family over the weekend. Rusty grumbled, "Don't let the brothers and sisters on the management team hear you say that. They aren't big fans of Larry. They have not forgiven him for saying that *discrimination against Black people is the same as discrimination against homosexuals.* That pissed-off a lot of Black people. They wondered what Larry was trying to say about Black people. They don't trust him."

Larry's statement, equating discrimination against Black people with discrimination against homosexuals, did seem a little bizarre, but I waited until I was alone with Larry to ask him to clarify what he meant.

Larry got a serious look on his face and said, "It's very simple. The psychology of discrimination works the same way, in the brain." Larry stared directly into my eyes. I think I understood what it was that Larry was trying to say, but I felt that there was a major flaw in his thesis.

"Larry," I said, "if a stranger walks into a room, in most cases you won't know whether that stranger is homosexual or not, unless he or she *tells* you. But when a Black stranger walks into a room, everybody will know that the stranger is Black, and any unconscious biases towards Black people will be triggered."

Larry thought about what I said then defiantly responded, "Nope, no difference!" I suspect that Larry was trying to describe how discrimination works, but the way he phrased it, especially in front of a woke Black audience, was bad optics.

My conversation with Larry was just one more indication of how complicated race had become. Even a well-meaning, self-described White liberal could be considered suspect by woke Black people.

—57—

"Shining Star"
Earth, Wind & Fire

Having Gloria's kid brother Ricky living with us was fun. The three of us moved into an 18th floor, three-bedroom, co-op apartment on 48th and Lake Park, with a nice view of Lake Michigan. Ricky did well academically, socially and athletically. He was an Honor student, a starter on Kenwood's football team and he had a great group of friends, Black and White. Even my close friends were impressed with Ricky, as were my parents.

Ricky had excellent high school grades, and he was accepted at several colleges. He got a scholarship and settled on Notre Dame. White people in Chicago had much respect for Notre Dame. Among Blacks, however, Notre Dame got mixed reviews, probably because many Blacks did not realize just how many Black students were attending the school other than members of Notre Dame's basketball and football teams.

Ricky told me that whenever he told people that he was going to school at Notre Dame but not playing football, they could not understand why he was there. Ricky would have to explain that Notre Dame was also an excellent academic institution.

Taking Rick to college for the first time in the fall of 1975 was exciting. Notre Dame's campus was beautiful, and the famous Word of Life mural, perhaps better known as "Touchdown Jesus," that adorned the façade of the largest on-campus college library in America, looked glorious.

Ricky moved into a double dormitory room and had three roommates, all of them White. One of them, Tom, was a normal-sized person from Oak Park, Illinois. But his other two roommates were basketball players, who towered five-feet-seven-inches and over Ricky by more than a foot.

One of Ricky's tall roommates was named Bruce Flowers, and the other was Bill Laimbeer, who went on to play in the National Basketball Association (NBA), where he was a four-time All Star and won two NBA Championships with the Detroit Pistons.

Laimbeer went on to coach in the Women's NBA (WNBA), where (so far) he has won three WNBA Championships and has been voted as WNBA Coach of the Year, twice.

Ricky got along well with most people, Black or White, but he never got along with Laimbeer. He told me that he and Laimbeer got into a "pissing match" one day and nearly came to blows, with Ricky standing on a table in order to be at eye level with Laimbeer. Eventually, Ricky moved to another room in the dorm. Laimbeer transferred to some other college before entering the NBA. Ricky graduated from Notre Dame in four years, earning a degree in Accounting.

Right after Ricky graduated from college in June 1979, he and I moved my friend, Billy Armstead, to Sacramento, California. Billy put his wife and three children on a plane and flew them to California, and then he rented a truck that Billy, Ricky and I loaded with Billy's furniture and drove across the country to Sacramento. It was like a "buddy" trip, my gift to Ricky for his graduation from college.

Ricky went to work for a large accounting firm, Peat, Marwick and Mitchel in Chicago, and after living with Gloria and me for seven years, he moved into his own apartment. He got married and moved to Houston, Texas, and now that Gloria and I live in Houston, we see Ricky at least once every week. *Just like ol times!*

—58—

"Flowers for Albert"
David Murray Octet

Despite Rusty's assessment, I did not regard my boss, Larry, as untrustworthy or a bad guy for comparing Black people with homosexuality. I just thought he was misguided. Apparently, some of the Whites in management did not like Larry much. One day, I overheard two White managers at the water cooler, criticizing Larry for "always trying to look like one of the Kennedys...with that shock of hair and his liberal ideas." Larry's unpopularity must have extended to the higher-ups at J&J, because I came in one day and was told that Larry had "resigned."

Larry's sudden departure turned out to be fortuitous for me. HR was reorganized and I was moved into Labor Relations. During the time that I was Manager of Wage and Salary and Benefits Administration, I learned a lot about the wage and benefits provisions contained in the Union contract, and I managed to develop rapport with Union leaders. So the Director of Industrial Relations, a White guy named West, promoted me to Manager of Labor Relations. In my new position, I primarily oversaw the administration of the Grievance Procedure and was the Company's spokesperson.

During my 2nd shift on an evening in March 1976, race was at the forefront of an incident that occurred in the plant. A young White, well-liked Production Supervisor named Dave found himself in the middle of a situation with racial overtones. Dave, who had an especially good relationship with the team of eight Black employees, was a recent graduate from the University of Michigan, and he especially enjoyed discussing college basketball with the department's Material Handler, Keenan, who, coincidentally, was about the same age as Dave.

Aware that the University of Michigan was one of the teams playing in the NCAA Final Four game that night, both Dave and Keenan expressed how much they wished they could see the game on TV. Responding, Dave told Keenan that he would excuse him for the night, if and when he supplied enough materials to the production lines to last the entire shift. Keenan's face lit up, and he and Dave shook hands on the deal. Keenan did not tell his co-workers about his and Dave's deal, he just kept working, feverishly through "lunch."

In the meanwhile, Dave joined two other White supervisors, who were his close friends, at lunch and mentioned the "deal" he had made with Keenan. Immediately, the other supervisors verbally attacked Dave for doing something so risky. One of the supervisors warned Dave that "if White employees to find out that you did a favor for a Black employee, they will be upset and want to know why there is no affirmative action for White employees."

Both of his friends advised Dave that he should get to Keenan, immediately, and tell him that the deal was off, and he could not leave early. Alarmed at his friends' warning, Dave left them in the cafeteria and hurried back into the plant to find Keenan.

In the meantime, Dave's friends were discussing Dave's predicament, and some of Keenan's co-workers overheard the supervisors talking. When Keenan's co-workers heard that Dave was going to renege on his deal with Keenan, they decided to support Keenan by staging a work stoppage: each of Keenan's co-workers would claim that he had received an "emergency phone call," requiring that he "come home, right away."

The alleged calls were spaced about fifteen minutes apart, and in the span of 90 minutes, each of Keenan's co-workers left the Plant, and the Department was forced to shut down.

The next morning, Dave's boss, the plant superintendent, complained that when the employees found out that Dave had reneged on his deal with Keenan, they had received "emergency phone calls" and left the plant and the department had been forced to shut down.

When a union employee resorts to "self-help" instead of using the "grievance procedure," it is a violation of the collective bargaining agreement and can result in discharging the employees who participate. The superintendent wanted me to fire the employees who had participated in the work stoppage.

I decided that I would build a case against the participants by requiring them to verify the "emergency" that caused them to have to leave the plant.

I knew that I had to be careful, because some of them may have, in fact *had* an "emergency." One employee's wife, for example, really was pregnant and may have been due to have the baby. But as I reviewed the alleged "emergency" each employee had claimed, I did not see an "emergency" listed for Keenan.

When I asked Dave why there was no "emergency" recorded for Keenan, I discovered that Dave had not "reneged" on his "deal" with Keenan at all. By the time Keenan's co-workers were hearing that Dave had reneged, Keenan had finished his work and left the plant.

Dave had kept his bargain with Keenan and excused him when Keenan's work was finished. Keenan did not need to stage an "emergency call." The misunderstanding concerning Keenan's status had occurred because Dave's friends, the two supervisors, were so sure that their warning to Dave about the danger of White employees' backlash to affirmative action had convinced Dave to renege on the deal.

This case taught me that a perilous racial situation does not always have villains. Everyone involved in this case was trying to do the right thing. Dave was trying to do a nice thing for Keenan; his friends, the two White supervisors, were trying to head-off what they worried would be severe, white backlash; and, last, but not least, Keenan's co-workers, were trying to bring attention to what they perceived to be an injustice. I ended up putting "warning letters" in Keenan's coworker's files and getting the Plant Manager to issue a memorandum clarifying "affirmative action." The way I handled the case resulted in my career at J&J getting a boost. My bosses praised me for "keeping the lid on" inside a plant located in a community with a history of tense race relations. And the Plant Management was happy that they did not have to hire and train a whole new crew. A short time later, I was promoted. That is when I also decided to add to my credentials by going to B-school.

—59—

"Wantu Wazuri, Use Afro Sheen...Beautiful People, Use Afro Sheen"
Donny Hathaway, Eulaulah Hathaway, Vince Cullers

The period between 1976 to 1980 was an especially exciting time for me and my family. Gloria gave birth to our first child, our son, Marcus, and we bought our first house. White people had not completely fled the East Beverly neighborhood where we bought, but the neighborhood was quickly turning Black. There was one White family on our block when we moved in and one interracial couple across the street, but everyone else on our block was Black. In 1980, our daughter, Kristin, was born.

Toward the end of 1980, Sandy, the same headhunter who got me into J&J, called me about "an extraordinary opportunity" she thought that might interest me as Director of Human Resources for Johnson Products Company (JPC), the Black-owned, publicly traded, Chicago-based hair care company, best known for Ultra Sheen and Afro Sheen and sponsoring *Soul Train*, the popular, TV dance program. The idea of working at a publicly traded, Black-owned company was a move I had not seen coming.

As intriguing as the JPC opportunity sounded, I still needed to be convinced that it would be a sound career move. I had been at J&J for nearly ten years, my career was going well, and I was only six months away from being vested in J&J's retirement plan. I had questions about whether working for a Black-owned would help or hurt my career? I also had questions about my fit at a Black company.

One of the reasons I had doubts about fitting in at JPC was that in the eleven years that I had worked in corporate America and gone to professional seminars, I had never seen anyone from a Black-owned firm attending the seminar. I always wondered how Black-owned companies keep up with the latest thinking in managing people. For me, to seriously consider working at JPC, I would have to get past my concerns that Black companies might be no more than ma and pa businesses on steroids.

Once again, it was my buddy Rusty who gave me perspective on Johnson Products. When I told him my concerns about Black-owned companies, Rusty reminded me that Johnson Products were publicly traded, so they "had to be professional." I also listened to what Sandy had to say about "fit" at Johnson Products, since her background was a lot like mine: Sandy had gone to B-school, and she had worked in management at a Fortune 500 company. When she looked me in the eye and told me that she thought I could fit at Johnson Products, I believed her.

One of the first things I picked up on that I found unique about JPC was that I only was interviewed by the person I would be reporting to, Dorothy McConner, JPC's tireless, 50-something, Executive Vice President. When Mrs. McConner told me she wanted to "hire someone who would bring Human Resources Management at Johnson Products into the 20th century," I was impressed, not because she talked about the 20th century, but because she referred to human resources management instead of "personnel."

In preparing for my interview at JPC, I did a little research on George Johnson, the founder and President of Johnson Products. One of the things I learned was that, as a young man, Johnson had worked for Fuller Cosmetic Products Company and its legendary founder and entrepreneur, S.B. Fuller, a Black man my father admired and often talked about.

Fuller was a proponent of self-help, and he maintained that race was not an insurmountable obstacle for Black people, so long as they had something to offer the World. Like Fuller, George Johnson did not go far in school, and like Fuller, Johnson began by selling cosmetics and personal care products, door-to-door. Johnson worked in the laboratory at Fuller's, where he rose to the position of Head Production Chemist and developed a hair relaxer for Black men.

When Mr. Johnson struck out on his own, he secured a loan and started Johnson Products Company. He developed Ultra Sheen, a hair straightener for Black women, and he generated a million dollars in sales in 1964. He then developed Afro Sheen. JPC grew to $12 million in sales. In 1971, JPC became the first Black-owned firm to trade on the American Stock Exchange.

The thing I found most compelling about George Johnson's

leadership was the way the firm had remained relevant and competitive as Black culture evolved from Negroes with "conked" hair" or "relaxed" hair, to Black People with "naturals" and Afros. In a way, it was possible to gain insight into Black history by tracking the evolution of Black hair care products at Johnson Products Company.

At the end of my interview with Mrs. McConner, she offered me the job at a very competitive salary. I told her that I would get back with her within a day. That night, when I discussed JPC's offer with Gloria, she told me to do whatever I thought was best for me. She made it clear that she did not have concerns about me leaving J&J so close to being vested, nor did she have concerns about me working for a Black-owned organization. She also told me told me she trusted Rusty and Sandy's judgment. The next day, I called Mrs. McConner and accepted the job.

—60—

"...You one of them technical niggas...You'll have problems here"
Nikki Giovanni, "Conversations"

When I started at Johnson Products in 1972, my first revelation was that the management team was diverse. JPC's Corporate Counsel was a Black woman, the Chief Financial Officer (CFO) was a White man, the VP of Operations was a Sikh from India, the Head of Research was Egyptian, and the Plant Manager was a Black woman. JPC had nearly 400 employees worldwide, including an operation in Lagos, Nigeria.

As soon as I started at JPC, I began looking for ways to have an impact and start the process of bringing JPC's human resources management into the 20th century. I only had to wait until the end of my first week at JPC to identify a way to have an impact.

At every place where I had ever worked, the employees got paid every two weeks. At Johnson Products, however, employees got paid every week. The payroll department was part of HR, so I was able to observe, up close, how difficult it was for the payroll administrator to produce the weekly payroll, while working to correct the previous week's errors.

After witnessing the stress of maintaining a weekly payroll system, I proposed that JPC change to a bi-weekly payroll schedule. I ran my idea past the CFO, and he said, "That's doable... I'm fine with the idea."

Later, when I told Ms. McConner that the CFO had said that going to a bi-weekly payroll was doable, she gushed, "That is exactly the kind of thinking I hoped you would bring to Johnson Products. Be sure to let Mr. Johnson know about the change you're proposing."

Two days later, I met with Mr. Johnson in his beautiful office. He greeted me warmly and opened our meeting by telling me that Ms. McConner had already informed him that I was proposing that JPC change to a bi-weekly payroll. Then, in a somber tone, Mr.

Are There Black Neighborhoods in Heaven? 185

Johnson asked, "George, do you know why I pay our employees every week?" Thinking that Mr. Johnson's question was rhetorical, I leaned forward in my chair, but did not answer.

"George, I pay our employees every week because Black people always need money!" I nearly laughed out loud at the profundity of what Mr. Johnson said to me. *Wow! I thought, they don't teach that in B-school, or seminars.*

Since most of JPC's employees were Black, I was sensitive about coming across as "one of them technical niggas," as Nikki Giovanni put it. Mr. Johnson showed me another way of looking at "weekly pay," So I remained quiet for a while, studying the lay of the land and did not propose any changes.

Then, a month after my conversation with Mr. Johnson, I decided to initiate another change. Realizing that there did not seem to be many hard and fast rules about compensation, JPC had pay inequities all over the place, so I tried to introduce a wage and salary structure and job evaluation system.

Mr. Johnson and Mrs. McConner bought into the structure and job evaluation system, and the management made a good faith effort to adhere to the structure. Occasionally, a manager would push back, as when a member of the executive team became impatient when I pointed out to him that he was not using the system correctly and he pounded his desk and yelled at me, "Goddammit, George, I am the system!"

Another time, I argued with Mr. Johnson's son, who was a sales director, about a large pay increase he wanted to give a saleswoman. After several minutes of arguing with me, Mr. Johnson's son got up from his chair, walked over to a window and pointed at the Johnson Products Company sign that was on the side of the building and, in a sarcastic tone, said, "Whose name do you see on this building?"

While I was pondering how I could persuade Mr. Johnson's son to get in line with the job evaluation system, I told Mrs. McConner about my confrontation with him. She told me to that she would speak with Mr. Johnson about the matter, "because of the sensitivity involved in dealing with the owner's son."

Later that day, Mrs. McConner came to my office with a serious look on her face. "Well," she said, glumly, "I spoke with Mr. Johnson about how his son reacted to you questioning how much his son wanted to pay someone, and what do you think he said?"

As I braced for the sting of Mr. Johnson's rebuke, Mrs. McConner's eyes narrowed, and a frown creased her brow. Then speaking deliberately, Mrs. McConner said, "Mr. Johnson told me, 'Dorothy, you tell George Smith that the quickest way for him to get fired from this company is to do anything that my son wants him to do without checking." She smirked and shook her head. I may have shaken my head too.

Things settled down considerably after my first year at JPC as the organization got used to my way of managing human resources. One of the things I was most proud of while at JPC was putting together a healthcare program where I brought in experts in healthcare, finance, benefits, law and education.

I brought in doctors, dentists, a school psychologist and a school administrator to present information and make themselves available to meet with individuals privately, until 7p.m. Even people from the neighborhood who were not JPC employees sneaked in and asked questions in the seminar. The program was so popular that other small business owners in the neighborhood and some church congregations as well asked if JPC would do the program again, but we never did.

As an aside, another thing I felt good about at JPC had to do with exposing Black people to jazz. Driving to lunch one day with Grayson Mitchell, the Director of Corporate Communications at Johnson Products, a tune called *Peaceful Heart and Gentle Spirit*, by flautist Chico Freeman, was playing on a cassette tape that I had mixed. Grayson had never heard the tune before, and he raved about it. A few weeks later, I heard the tune playing in the background of a JPC ad that aired on a popular Black radio station. Hearing *Peaceful Heart and Gentle*

Members of The Jazz Fraternity with Wynton Marsalis and pianist Marcus Roberts. My buddy Ron Chears is in the left and I am behind Wynton on the right.

Spirit on the radio ranked right up there with the things of which I was most proud.

—61—

"By the time you realize that your father was right, you'll have a son of your own..."
(Unknown)

As my son, Mark, was growing up, I tried to guide and mentor him the same way that my father had mentored me about race. When I was a kid, I got tired of hearing my father talk about race all the time and a lot of what he had to say about race went in one ear and out the other. Once I started going to school with White kids, however, my father's comments about race seemed to increase in intensity and urgency. The older I got, the more I discovered how those things he had to say about race really did apply to me, whether I wanted to see or hear it that way or not. Once I had children of my own, I wanted their awareness about race to evolve in much the same way it had for me.

When I started at Johnson Products, I lived in East Beverly, only a few miles from JPC's corporate offices, and my son, Mark, attended an integrated neighborhood public school. We were able to get him into Beasley Academy, a magnet school that pulled in kids from all over Chicago, including White kids. Beasley is located near the working-class poor all-Black neighborhood where I grew up. Beasley though, was a magnet school and the public elementary school of choice for many upwardly mobile Black professionals.

Race was never an issue at Beasley, but gender very nearly was. When Mark was in 3rd grade, one of his old teachers called to warn us that she had heard that Mark was one of three Black boys to earn academic excellence awards, but two female 3rd grade teachers were planning to award only two of the boys and give the third award to a girl, because the optics would look better. The teacher who called us told to me take our concerns to the Assistant Principal, which we did. Luckily, the Assistant Principal headed off the problem, and all the boys, including Mark, received their awards.

In 1985, Gloria and I moved from Beverly to Oak Park, IL, a near-West Chicago suburb, known for its excellent, integrated public schools. My daughter, Kris, at five, was just entering Kindergarten, and nine-year-old Mark was going into fourth grade. Both of my kids adapted quickly to life in mostly White Oak Park. We wanted our children in Oak Park because we thought it would help them gain a healthy perspective on race.

Mark's evolution was sometimes painfully slow. He was naïve and stubborn and pushed back whenever I brought up race. He once asked me, *Why do you always add a person's race to that person's description? Like if somebody's at our front door, you don't just say there is a man at the front door— you'll say there is a White man at the front door. Why do you do that?* I could not think of a profound response, so I simply said, "Because it's important."

My daughter, Kris, on the other hand, developed much better instincts regarding race than Mark. When she was seven, Kris told her mother that she wanted "flappy hair...like the White girls." Worried that Kris might be going through an identity crisis and feeling that the quality of White hair was superior to her own, we agreed that Gloria should have a heart-to-heart talk with Kris. But our concerns proved to be unfounded. Kris wanted "flappy hair like the white girls" because White hair is easier to manage after swimming. That's when I realized that Black women and men approach race differently.

From the moment he was born, Mark was physically precocious. As a baby, he turned himself over in his crib, the week after he was born. He stood up on his own at six months, and he walked by himself when he was seven months old. He could toss a baseball over his head and catch it before he was two years old. Mark developed a love of sports including basketball, football and baseball at an early age. Oak Park had a strong youth sports program, and Mark excelled in both youth football and baseball.

My son, Marcus.
This book is dedicated to him.

In 1989, when Mark was thirteen, Oak Park Youth Baseball League assembled a team to compete in the Bronco League World Series in Sacramento, California. The Oak Park Youth Bronco League consisted of six teams and about 75 kids, including a total of seven Black kids. All the coaches were White men.

Mark had been among the better ballplayers that summer, so after two days of trying out for the World Series Team, I was surprised that Mark had not been among the first kids announced as having been selected to the team.

On the last day of try-outs, I decided to drop by the ballfield where the tryouts were being held to offer Mark encouragement. As I got out my car in the parking lot just before the tryouts began for the day, I happened to see one of the coaches. When I asked the coach how Mark was faring in the tryouts, the coach looked around nervously and gestured for me to come closer. "Look," he whispered, "I think Mark should be alright... it's just that the Commissioner does not want to end up with too many Blacks on the team...but you didn't hear that from me."

Mark made the team. Nevertheless, I was reminded that race was already playing a big role in his young life. Mark was one of the three Black kids to make the team, but I was the only Black parent to make the trip to Sacramento to watch the Oak Park team compete in the World Series.

The parents of the two other Black kids on the team asked me if their sons could stay in the hotel room with Mark and me, and I told them they could. One of the White kids whose parents did not make the trip, stayed in our room as well.

None of the Black kids played much in the Series, but Mark did make a game-saving catch. On a day when there were no games being played, I visited with Armstead at his home in Sacramento, while a group of Oak Park families rented a van and drove to San Francisco to do sight-seeing. Mark opted to ride in the van to San Francisco. Later I learned that Mark had done an amazing job, acting as the group's tour guide. Even more remarkable, he had previously only been to San Francisco once.

—62—
"Rag, Bush and All"
Henry Threadgill

By 1988, I felt that I had gone as far as I could go at Johnson Products Company, so I began to consider leaving. I had no regrets about my six years at JPC, but I wanted more responsibility and more money. So when an opportunity presented itself in Chicago's burgeoning healthcare industry, I took it, landing a position as Director of Human Resources at Bethany Hospital.

Bethany was one of six major hospitals in and around the Chicago area. Bethany Hospital was the smallest hospital in the system, but it was in a new building in an all-Black neighborhood on the West Side, fifteen minutes from Oak Park. I viewed healthcare as one of the most stable industries for my career. My plan was to work at Bethany for a couple years and move to one of the larger hospitals in the system, perhaps working my way into becoming Vice President of HR for the entire system.

My first boss at Bethany, was the President of the hospital, a White man named Ken with a white beard and a twinkle in his eye. We developed an instant rapport. Early in my employment, Ken, hipped me to the fact that Bethany's drug rehab unit was filled with wealthy White people who were "hiding where none of their White friends would think to look for them," as they underwent rehab.

Under Ken's leadership, I enjoyed my work and learned the healthcare industry. After I had been at Bethany for about a year, Ken retired. His replacement was an impressive brother from Ohio named Brown, who I grew to like. But when I looked at the other hospitals in the system, I realized that HR was in the hands of smart and experienced White men and women who had all been in the system longer than me. Vice President of HR for the entire system seemed too far away. I stayed at Bethany another year, and then left.

—63—

"One line, Two views"
Muhal Richard Abrams

When you grow up in Chicago, you are never more than a mile or two from railroad tracks. I loved trains, probably because I grew up riding them so much, mostly to Springfield, Illinois, my favorite place in the World. In Springfield, not only did I get to spend a lot of time with my grandfather, but I also got to play with my cousins, Joyce and Donald.

Donald was seven years older and had an electric train set on a large piece of plywood. I would watch, in awe as Donald's Lionel train went around that board and a toy conductor would emerge from a little house with a lantern that glowed. I grew up wanting a model railroad set just like Donald's, but whenever I would tell my mother that I planned to ask Santa Claus for a train, she would say, "You'd better wait until next year, when you get a little older." I never got that train set.

Anytime I felt like I needed a model railroad fix, I would ask my parents if we could visit the Museum of Science and Industry, where I would marvel at the Museum's 3500 square-foot Model Railroad Exhibit. The Museum had no admission charge in those days, so my family visited the museum often.

The Museum offered a wonderland of exhibits and interactives to keep me, my sister and my parents engaged for the entire day. On some Sundays, we would even have dinner in the Museum's dining room. In the days before Disneyland and Disney World, the Museum of Science and Industry was a memorable experience for the whole family.

The Museum of Science and Industry (MSI) was established in 1933 and occupied what had been the Palace of Fine Arts at the 1893 World's Columbian Exposition, next to Lake Michigan, between Jackson Park and the University of Chicago. The Museum has long been regarded as one of the world's great museums. So, when a headhunter called me in 1991 and said the Museum was looking for a Director of Human Resources, there was never any question in my mind that I wanted a shot at that job.

Working at the Museum would come as close as any place I could imagine as a dream job. I loved the idea that I would be working with smart people, engaged in creating memorable, science-based experiences for visitors, just like the Model Railroad exhibit had been for me when I was a kid.

To get the job at the Museum, I only had to interview with two people, both White men. The Vice President of Operations and the President and CEO. Todd, the VP of Operations, to whom I would report, was a Molecular Biologist. The President of the Museum, Jack Kahn, was a geophysicist who had come to the Museum from Lawrence Livermore Laboratories in California. I sensed both interviews had gone well, but it was still thrilling when Todd called and offered me the position.

*****

Months before I started at the museum, an admission fee schedule was put on the door for the first time in its 60-year history. MSI had long been an extraordinary science museum and visitor experience, but it needed revenue to help develop new exhibits and programs to be competitive with Chicago's other iconic cultural institutions, including the Field's Museum of Natural History, the Art Institute, The Shedd Aquarium and The Adler Planetarium.

The Museum was also building an underground parking garage, so a source of revenue was needed. Todd and Jack concluded that charging admission would raise the public's demand for a higher quality of customer service as part of the museum experience, so Todd initiated a Total Quality Management (TQM program) as the way to optimize "the museum experience." Managing human resources in a TQM environment turned out to be a great way for me to learn the museum business.

Despite his brilliance, Todd was a "little different" socially. He and I had enlightening discussions on a variety of subjects, and he was even into esoteric stuff, like yoga. The one thing that I found unsettling about Todd, who was married, was the way he constantly ogled women. He thought nothing of telling me how sexy he found some women to be.

When he did that, I never knew how to react. Once, when Todd and I were meeting in his office, he asked his administrative assistant, Marge, a blonde-haired White woman, to bring him a file. Marge came in and placed the file on Todd's desk, and as she turned to walk out of Todd's office, I noticed that he stopped talking and watched her walk out. Then when she closed the door behind her, Todd said, "I find her very attractive."

When I did not say anything, Todd added, "That's a problem I have..." As a Black man, I was never sure how to handle a situation in which a White man was ogling a White woman and trying to get a reaction out of me. After all, Black men have been killed for less.

One Friday afternoon, after Todd asked me if I had plans for the weekend, I told him that I was planning to drive my mother to Kokomo, Indiana, for the "Artis Family Reunion." A bemused look came over Todd's face. "That's interesting," he said, "I once had a very dear friend from Kokomo, Indiana. Her name was June Artis. She was a very beautiful woman." Todd's eyes glazed over, and I could not be sure if I told him that a June Artis was hosting the Reunion.

When my mother and I arrived at the Artis Family Reunion, the first person we met was June Artis. June looked to be in her 50s, and she *was* pretty. When I told June that I worked with Todd at the Museum of Science and Industry, she smiled coyly and said, "You and I need to talk before you leave here today." Unfortunately, June was busy during the reunion, so she and I never had a chance to talk, but as Mom and I were leaving, June and I promised to stay in touch. We never did.

When I got back to the office on Monday, Todd and I walked into the Museum together, and he immediately asked me if I had made it to the Artis Family Reunion and met June. I told him I had met June, and she seemed like a nice lady. But that's all I said, as Todd stared off into space.

—64—

"Wayne's Trane"
Ari Brown

I continued learning and things went well for me in my first two years at the museum. One morning, as I came to work, my Assistant, Renetta, told me that Dr. Kahn, the President, wanted to see me in his office as soon as I arrived.

I rushed over to Jack's office and noticed his assistant, Eileen, with a silly grin on her face. He saw me enter his suite and beckoned me into his office.

After shutting the door and bidding me to sit down, Jack sat on the edge of his desk directly in front of me, extending a handshake as he said, "Congratulations. You're now the Vice President for Human Resources and Administration for the Museum of Science and Industry. I accepted Todd's resignation, and the Board approved your promotion to Vice President. Your responsibilities will be essentially the same as Todd's, but I am changing the job title to VP of HR and Administration' because, honestly, I've never liked the title of Chief Operating Officer.

Jack clapped his hands, patted me on the back and congratulated me again. As I left his office, Eileen smiled and mouthed the words, "Congratulations." I was exactly where I wanted to be. Reporting directly to Jack was great. He was unassuming, yet decisive.

Yet despite his enormous intellect—or, perhaps because of it—Jack was able to relate to everyone on the staff, from ticket-takers, as he called them, to security guards to plumbers to the members of the executive team. He was passionate about science education, and creative.

From the start, Jack exhibited confidence in me and my abilities, frequently calling upon me to facilitate senior management team meetings and asking me to weigh in on tough issues. I was in the best job I ever had. Jack allowed me to lead and initiate change, and he encouraged me to keep up strong relationships in the community, including the Black community.

Things were going well, making me feel I had floated through my first year as VP. Although I inherited parts of the Museum's underground parking garage project, staff development continued to be my primary role in HR. I was happy at the museum.

I sensed that the Museum would be the last move of my career. Consequently, I was in shock on the day Jack told me he had decided to retire to his second home in Galena, Illinois. He laughed and said that he was planning to manage a Mexican restaurant he had bought in Galena, an historic, small town 160 miles northwest of Chicago, famous for being the one-time, home of Civil War hero and former President, General Ulysses S. Grant.

I was sad to see Jack leave but not all that surprised. At 66, he was spirited and eager to take on his "next challenge." He had made a big difference in my life, and I would miss him.

All of us on the Museum's Senior Management team began to talk about who we thought would succeed Jack. Everybody figured his successor would come from outside the organization and would be a scientist or a science education heavyweight.

Among those of us on the Senior Management team, there was considerable speculation that the museum's next president would come from NASA, since Jack had worked so closely with NASA in the development of the museum's Space Shuttle Experience, the museum's most recent exhibit and experience.

In fact, one popular name being tossed around the management team as a candidate to become the museum's next president was Dr. Mae Jemison, the Black, female astronaut who was a product of Chicago's Public Schools. Dr. Jemison checked all the boxes, and several of us on the senior management team, myself included, thought she would be an exciting choice for president. I was eager to work with someone like Dr. Jemison, but I was also confident I would be able to work with anybody from the academic or scientific community.

Absolutely no one on the senior management team expected the next president of the Museum of Science and Industry to come from City of Chicago government, especially someone who had been on the mayor's staff. In fact, hardly any of us on the Executive Team knew anything about the new president of the Museum.

Even though he was not as bombastic as his father, Mayor

Richard J. Daley had been, I always had an uneasy feeling about Mayor Richard M. Daley. My buddy Doc's law firm had done business with the city, and I remember him telling me that Richard M. was "not that bad."

But I always wondered about Richard M., who succeeded Chicago's first two Black Mayors, Harold Washington and Eugene Sawyer, and who openly campaigned that the people of Chicago preferred a White mayor. I had a hard time imagining how anyone who had been on the mayor's staff would be someone with whom I could find synergy. But I intended to try.

—65—

"Beware Greeks bearing gifts, colored men asking for a loan and white men who understand the Negro."
Adam Clayton Powell

My challenges with the new president began even before his first official day at the museum. The museum's Director of Business Affairs, a White woman named Nancy, told me that she had agreed to rent the museum's ballroom to a Black men's social club for a huge party.

Nancy rented the museum ballroom as often as she could, but this time, after agreeing to the deal, Nancy found out through a Black woman on her staff that the club had a bad reputation for wild parties that "got out of hand," with drinking, drugging and fighting. Nancy decided to cancel the event and refund the club its deposit.

Nancy's boss, the VP of Finance, who was also White, told Nancy that "cancelling the event was a bad idea, because it might offend the Black community." But when she asked my opinion, I told her I agreed that she should cancel the event and refund the money. She asked if I would talk with her boss, and I agreed.

Before I met with the VP, I ran the matter past a brother who I knew would be familiar with the club, and he confirmed that the crowd that the club would attract posed a bad risk for a place like the museum, with its interactive exhibits and precious artifacts.

When I told the VP that I agreed with Nancy's plan to cancel the party for security reasons, he offered, "I think that canceling the event might offend the Black community."

I responded that the Black community was not monolithic, and while some Black people may not appreciate that the event was cancelled, most Black people do not like rowdy parties, and they would understand the museum's decision to cancel. The VP was not confrontational, and he seemed to be enjoying our friendly jousting. He paused for a few seconds to think about what I had said, and then he laughed, saying, "Hey, I am expecting a call later today from our new 'fearless leader,' the new president, so why don't we let him decide. Let him start earning those big bucks. When he calls me, I'll plug you in and we can have a three-way conversation."

An hour later, the VP of Finance plugged me into the call from the new president, who echoed the same sentiment about "not offending the Black community." I told the president that I appreciated his concerns about offending the Black community, but based on what I had learned about the club, I doubted that the broader Black community would be offended.

The president pondered the matter for a moment, then snickered, "Hey, why are we arguing? Heck, I'm not even there yet. You guys decide." And the call ended.

The VP of Finance and I discussed the matter a little longer, but neither of us changed our position. Since museum security reported to me, I took charge and declared the event a "security risk," advising Nancy to cancel the event and refund the money. I did not realize it at the time, but my insistence that the event be canceled was probably "strike one" against me as far as the new president was concerned.

None of my efforts to engage with the new president were ever successful. For example, when he told me that he served on the Board of the Lab School, I told him that I had attended the Lab School, back in the 1950s and would love to chat with him about how things may have changed for Black students since I was there. That conversation never happened. Another time, the new president told me that he lived on 57th and Kimbark, right next door to William Ray School, and I told him, "Wow, what a coincidence! Gloria— my wife, Gloria is the School Psychologist at Ray." No reaction.

*****

In my first couple years at MSI with Jack Kahn's encouragement, I cultivated a good relationship with the University of Chicago's Jazz Institute, even co-sponsoring a couple jazz concerts in the museum's auditorium. So, when the Jazz Institute called to tell me that vocalist Kurt Elling, a rising, White, international jazz star and Hyde Park resident, wanted to do a free outdoor concert next to the lagoon behind the museum, I went to the new president, seeking his approval. The new president response was, "That's Chicago Park District property behind the museum. Make sure you get permission from the Chicago Park District, the local Alderwoman and all the players in the community before you go ahead with the event." I assured him that I would.

The guy I spoke with at the Park District laughed and said he did not even know that the lagoon was Park District property. He said that the Park District had no problem with a concert. Then, I spoke with the local Alderwoman, who said she would have no problem with the concert. "Sounds nice," she chuckled, "I might even check out the concert."

Checking off the names of each one of the players, it did not appear that any of them had a problem with the concert. But before I reported back to the new president, I decided I had better check with the State Senator about the concert.

The State Senator was not available, but when I told his assistant the reason I was calling, she briefly put me on hold. She returned to tell me that the Senator was on his way to a meeting near the museum and to expect him in front of the museum in a "few minutes." She said I could ask him about the concert in person. I hurried out the museum and the State Senator showed-up, exactly when she said he would. He shook my hand and listened patiently to my pitch regarding the concert. The Senator said that he thought the concert was "a great idea" and he and his wife "might come by and listen to some jazz." He then continued to his meeting.

I went directly to Museum's president and told him that all "players were okay with the Museum doing the concert, even the State Senator." The new president scoffed, "Aww, he's not important."

That State Senator, of course, was Barack Obama.

—66—

"If I Break"
Al Jarreau

The Elling concert went off without a hitch and was well attended. Neither the State Senator nor the Alderwoman showed up, but more significantly, neither did the new president, who lived within walking distance of the lagoon. When I looked around and did not see the president, I knew it was strike two. Strike three occurred two months after the concert.

My colleague Jaimie, the museum's Vice President of Development, told me she was worried that the museum's best fundraiser, Ann, might resign because she was so frustrated with the president's role in fundraising.

I did not know anything about fundraising, but I gathered from what Jaimie was telling me that Ann's fundraising style required bringing the Museum President "in" at a certain point in the process, but the new president did not see that as his role. Jaimie said that she had discussed the matter with the new president, but she concluded "that he doesn't seem to get it." I told Jaimie I would see if I could help.

My plan was to meet with the president, outline the problem as Jamie had explained it to me, and then sit back and listen. I figured new president had sound reasons, based on his experiences and philosophy of fundraising, so I would be quiet and learn something. After meeting with him, I planned to convey his perspective to Jamie and Ann and help them devise a strategy for making their working relationship with the new president effective.

Rather than accuse him of being "the problem," I deliberately tried to be vague in my meeting with the president by talking in generalities about "getting everyone on the same page." But the president was having none of it.

He blew up my plan to gradually get into a discussion about fundraising philosophies and strategies when, suddenly, he pulled out a legal pad, slammed it on his desk and snarled, "Give me names! I want names!!" I was so unsettled by the hostility he showed that I apologized for coming into the meeting without names.

Trying to regroup, I told the president that I would reschedule a meeting and come back with "names." I had decided to encourage Jaimie to talk with the president herself. She could decide if she wanted to disclose names. But before I could get with Jaimie, the new president fired me. He did not give me a reason for firing me, except to say, "Things aren't working out!" That was it. My dream job was history.

My reaction to being fired was uncharacteristically muted and docile, because I was preoccupied and emotionally engaged in a matter involving my son, Mark, who was away from home at a major university on a baseball scholarship.

*****

In high school, Mark had been recruited to play collegiate baseball by several schools, and he chose Notre Dame. His career got off to a great start. He was the only freshman starting and one of four Black players in the starting lineup when the season opened. I traveled to several of the team's early games and saw Mark perform at a high level. His college baseball future seemed bright, he was happy and doing well in school.

Then suddenly Mark was replaced in the lineup by a White kid, who frankly was not nearly as skilled as Mark. When I asked Mark why he was not playing, he told me that he did not know. Even some of the parents in the stands, Black and White, seemed puzzled by Mark's removal from the lineup.

As the season went on. Mark never got back into the lineup, and by the end of his freshman year, he was depressed and disconsolate, and his grades began to sag. I asked the coach what Mark needed to work on to get more playing time, and his coach told me, "Mr. Smith, I don't think Mark will ever play much for me. His swing is too long and he strikes out too much. And besides hitting a baseball 500 feet from time to time, I am not impressed with his game."

I knew enough about baseball to know the shortcomings in Mark's 'game' that his coach mentioned could be corrected with practice and coaching, and that is what I told the coach. Finally, he replied, "Mr. Smith, if Marcus wants to come back here, I will renew his scholarship, and he can get this university's good education. But he will never play much for me." I concluded that Mark's coach, for whatever reasons, did not like Mark.

When I finished talking with the coach, I had the toughest conversation with Mark that I had ever had. I told him what his coach said and suggested to Mark that I did not think there was anything that he could do to change the coach's opinion of him. I suggested he might want to consider transferring to another college if he wanted to continue playing college baseball.

I saw the hurt and bewilderment in Mark's eyes, and as his father, I felt helpless that I could not erase the pain he was feeling. When I got fired from the Museum, Mark was on my mind more than my own situation.

Dad at age 86 and Mom at age 81 on the steps of the Museum of Science and Industry where they were part of "the senior walker's program."

—67—

"Pastime Paradise"
Stevie Wonder

Gloria, me, Mark and Kris, one of the last times we were all together.

To be sure, 1995 was a tough year in the Smith household, with Mark's problem at Notre Dame and my getting fired from the Museum. But Mark and I both landed on our feet. Mark did leave Notre Dame. He transferred to Michigan State University, another Division I Program, on a baseball scholarship, where he played every inning of every game for the next two and one-half years. Then he transferred to the University of Illinois in Champaign from which he graduated with a BS in Economics.

Mark had professional baseball aspirations and had hoped to use his last semester of college eligibility to play baseball as a graduate student. But a serious eye injury ended his professional aspirations. He went on to become a professional model, work in real estate and manage a hotel in Miami Beach, Florida.

After getting fired from the museum, I landed a good-paying job as HR Director for a specialized Nurse's Association in a Chicago suburb. I also taught both graduate and undergraduate classes in HR and Organization Behavior at the Lake Forest Graduate School of Management and at the Illinois Institute of Technology, and I started a consulting business.

One of my consulting clients was the Children's Museum in Indianapolis. In 1997, the National Collegiate Athletic Association (NCAA) moved its headquarters to Indianapolis (from Kansas City), and as a result of the work I had done for Children's Museum in 1998, the Chairwoman of the Children's Museum's Board put me in touch with the NCAA and recommended me.

After several interviews, the NCAA hired me to be Managing Director of The NCAA Hall of Champions, a museum-like gallery and special events venue. The NCAA was a great place to land.

My decision to move from Chicago to Indianapolis was a little tough, since my parents were older and living in a "senior's residence" in Chicago in a gentrified part of the city on 41st Street, near what had been the all-Black neighborhood where I had grown up. Middle-class White people were now living in condominium, transformed from the "six-flat" apartment buildings, full of poor, Black people from my childhood memories. Seeing White people jogging, pushing baby carriages and riding bikes on 41st Street was remarkable.

It was not until Barack Obama was elected President of the United States that my brain emerged from the fog of race that started in 1950, when I saw a Black Santa Claus for the first time. What dawned on me was that the White man who fired me from the Museum of Science and Industry in 1995 is the same White man who told me that Barack Obama was "not important."

He had been wrong about Obama— who was important enough to become President of the United States— and he had been wrong about me.

Don't misunderstand me, I am not comparing myself to Barack Obama, except to the extent that he and I are both intelligent, capable Black men who have been disparaged and marginalized by the same White man. Most White men cannot evaluate Black men. I think the museum president saw me and Barack Obama as feckless, "uppity Negroes," and White folks— especially White men, have always had a thing about "uppity Negroes."

The president of the Museum never told me the reason he fired me, except to say, "things aren't working out." I think he simply disliked me, for whatever the reason. And that's okay. It is okay for one human being to dislike another human being. At least, it qualifies me as a human being. (So, I have that going for me).

You may be surprised to learn that many White people never think of Black people as human beings. That's not as far-fetched as you might think, when you consider that, at one time, the Constitution counted Black people as 3/5 of a person. Years of not thinking of Black people as human beings is one of the things that has given rise to "unconscious bias."

I once taught an all-White class of college seniors at an urban university, and none of them knew that Black and White people can have the same blood type, except for one student who said, "I get it— same species."

Epilogue

"September"
Kirk Franklin

Tragically, we lost our son, Mark, in 2019. He died from a viral infection. He was 42 and lived in Miami Beach, Florida.

I feel that at the time of his death, Mark was beginning to understand race. Growing up, Mark was slow to grasp the vagaries of race, just as I had been when I was young. And my understanding of race came as the result of years of socialization, rather than a single moment of conversion. Like I said, as a kid, Mark pushed back whenever I suggested that a situation could be race-based. His attitude about race frustrated me, the same way my naiveté about race must have frustrated my father. But there were signs that Mark was coming around.

An indication that Mark's head was not completely buried in the sand regarding race took place in 2018, when a hurricane was approaching the southern tip of Florida. Mark's live-in girlfriend was White, and with the storm a day away from slamming into Florida, Mark and his girlfriend were trying to decide where they could go to escape the storm.

Mark's girlfriend wanted them to drive to a resort near Mobile, Alabama. Mark told me that he was "not comfortable" with going someplace like Alabama, where White people's reaction to an interracial couple might force him to act like an angry Black man." He said he preferred going to a place "with a history of seeing interracial couples." He and his girlfriend finally settled on a hotel in Orlando, Florida. I was relieved.

Mark never did buy-in to my conspiracy theory as to why he was benched by his first college baseball coach. And who knows, there may have been other reasons. Race could have been just *one* of them.

Acknowledgments

My wife, Gloria Smith.

My daughter, Kristin Smith-Clinton

My late parents, George O. And Lorrine Smith.

My late grandfather, Orville Artis, who told me our family's history.

My cousins, Marie, John and Allan Smith, and my late cousin, MacDonald's Jackson.

Tom Paulick, my first boss in corporate America.

Edith Stephens, who knew my great-great grandfather in Paris, Illinois, and took me to visit my great-great-great-grandfather's church in Charleston, Illinois.

Kathleen Carpenter, a dear friend.

Ari Brown, my old friend and an amazing musician.

Bill Rhoden, a dear friend who encouraged me and reminded me to "take the horn out of your mouth."

Paul Heinegg, *Free African Americans of North Carolina*, Third Edition, June 1992

www.ingramcontent.com/pod-product-compliance
Lightning Source LLC
Chambersburg PA
CBHW071703090426
42738CB00009B/1642